AMC
River Guide

MASSACHUSETTS
CONNECTICUT
RHODE ISLAND

AMC
River Guide

MASSACHUSETTS
CONNECTICUT
RHODE ISLAND

Second Edition

APPALACHIAN MOUNTAIN CLUB
BOSTON

Edited by Steve Tuckerman
Cover design by Joyce Weston

Library of Congress Cataloging-in-Publication Data

AMC river guide. Massachusetts, Connecticut, Rhode Island/edited by
    Steve Tuckerman—2nd ed.
        p.   cm.
    Includes index.
    ISBN 1-878239-00-7: $11.95
        1. Canoes and canoeing—Massachusetts—Guide-books. 2. Canoes and
canoeing—Connecticut—Guide-books. 3. Canoes and canoeing—Rhode
Island—Guide-books. 4. Massachusetts—Description and travel—1981- —Guide-
books. 5. Connecticut—Description and travel—1981- —Guide-books. 6. Rhode
Island—Description and travel—1981- —Guide-books. I. Tuckerman, Steve. II.
Appalachian Mountain Club. III. Title: Massachusetts, Connecticut, Rhode Island.
GV776.M4A43   1990
797.1'22—dc20   90-37338

SECOND EDITION
© 1985, 1990 by the Appalachian Mountain Club

Published by Appalachian Mountain Club Books, 5 Joy St., Boston, MA 02108.
Distributed by The Talman Company, 150 Fifth Ave., New York, NY 10011.

The paper used in this publication meets the minimum requirements of the American
National Standard for Information Sciences—Permanence of Paper for Printed Library
Materials, ANSI Z39.48-1984.

**Due to changes in conditions, use of the information in t
is at the sole risk of the user.**

Printed in the United States of America
10 9 8 7 6 5 4 3 2 1

90 91 92 93 94

CONTENTS

PREFACE

The first extensive guidebook to New England rivers was *Quickwater and Smooth*, by John C. Phillips and Thomas D. Cabot, published in 1935. In 1965, the Appalachian Mountain Club published its *New England Canoeing Guide*. This was an updated and greatly expanded version of the earlier work, assembled by a committee of volunteers under the direction of Kenneth Henderson and Stewart Coffin. Revised editions were published in 1968 and 1971.

The *New England Canoeing Guide*, in turn, was replaced by the AMC River Guide, a book with a format designed for easier reference. Separate volumes were published for northeastern and south-central New England, and the text was expanded. Updated river descriptions incorporated headings giving important characteristics of each river segment. The volunteer architect for this restructuring was Philip Preston.

Conversations with users disclosed that arbitrary political boundaries meant more to most canoeists than natural watershed boundaries, and so it was decided that subsequent editions of the *River Guide* would be organized according to state boundaries. The first *River Guide* that followed state lines was published in 1980, the *AMC River Guide: Maine*. The next volume, the *AMC River Guide: New Hampshire and Vermont*, was published in 1983 and updated in 1989. The first edition of this volume was prepared in 1985 under the able direction of Roioli Schweiker. The driving force behind this update has been Vera Smith, who put together an army of river checkers and followed up to ensure that the rivers were checked. Vera is stepping down as volunteer coordinator. She will be impossible to replace.

This edition reflects the advances in paddling that have taken place over recent years. Difficult rivers such as the West Branch of the Deerfield and the Cold are included for the first time. This edition also attempts to rate rivers based on modern interpretations.

Although there may be disagreement over some of the ratings, I have tried to be consistent. In addition, I have deleted differentiations between open and closed boats, as open boats can go anywhere a closed boat can.

Following is the list of river checkers; I thank them all. Special thanks go to George Ellmore, who makes flatwater sound interesting, to Steve Gephard, who discovered whitewater rivers within five miles of my former home, and to Jim Michaud, who pushed the outside of the envelope. Thanks also go to Joe Child for providing descriptions that made my palms sweat and for showing me the Cold River. Checkers were Trescott Abele, William Blaha, Ed Bossom, Paul Bumpus, Candy Carlisle, John Cary, David Low of the Charles River Watershed Association, Ed Chase, Joe Child, Russ Cohen, Carolyn Crowell, Bill Cushwa, Jim D'Attilio, Lise and Ken Denault, Rod Dore, Bob Eaton, George Ellmore, Mike Fullerton, Steve Gephard, John Harmon, Kent Heidenis, David Hodgdon, Al Howcroft and Nancy Hagstrom, Roger Jones, Jeanne Kangas, Jim Michaud, John O. Mitchell, Chris Ryan, Marlene Schroeder, David Shepard, Steve Sokoloski, Hank Stahr, Bob White, and David Williams. I also checked and wrote up rivers I knew.

In addition, I would like to thank all those who got me interested in paddling, who continue my advancement in paddling, and who just paddle with me from time to time.

And finally, special thanks go to my wife Krystyna, both for putting up with me and for her skills and enthusiasm on the rivers.

Steve Tuckerman

INTRODUCTION

Four major drainage basins in southern New England account for most of the rivers described in this guidebook. The Housatonic River drains western Massachusetts and western Connecticut, offering a variety of trips both on its main stem and its pleasant tributaries. The Connecticut River drains central Massachusetts and central Connecticut and offers flatwater on its main stem. Outstanding tributaries of the Connecticut include the Millers, the Deerfield, the Westfield with its branches, the Farmington, and the Salmon. The Thames River drains eastern Connecticut and a small portion of Rhode Island and Massachusetts. The best paddling in this area is found on the Willimantic and the Natchaug. And finally, the Merrimack River drains northeastern Massachusetts and central New Hampshire. There the Concord and Sudbury offer interesting flatwater trips.

The area between major drainage basins offers mostly flatwater trips. Suggested trips are the Wood, the Bass, and the Parker.

Many rivers in these watersheds have not been included because no current information could be found. To compound the confusion, the same river has different names in different sections and on different maps, and yet different local names. Gathering up-to-date information for this book was not easy, and unfortunately the line had to be drawn somewhere.

SAFETY

Although this book was prepared with care, no guidebook should be used on blind faith. Along with a map, it is a very helpful companion to have when you run a river, but it will not prevent every problem.

This book will not protect you from yourself. Managing a boat in current requires a degree of skill that depends on the nature of the river. Maneuvering with style and finesse is considerably different from just paddling hard. Sometimes paddling hard works, but the faster the current the less effective it is. Be realistic about your abilities and do not underestimate the power and difficulty of a river. The Safety Code of the American Whitewater Affiliation is included in the appendix; it contains many good suggestions for safe boating.

This book will also not protect you from unexpected rapids or obstacles. Many permanent changes in rivers have taken place within the last few decades, and they have often occurred when dams were washed out. New England still has many old dams that could collapse and expose whatever the millponds covered. There is always the possibility of encountering temporary or seasonal obstructions. Snowmobile bridges and ice-dam nets have become a noteworthy hazard on some small quickwater streams: they are low and often awash. They usually block a river even more effectively than a fallen tree.

And lastly, this book will not protect you from sudden changes in water level. A moderate spring or autumn rainfall will significantly affect a river with a large, mountainous watershed. In a matter of hours the river can rise several feet and so become more difficult and hazardous. Unanticipated releases from dams can have the same effect.

Boating, as a sport, involves certain risks that can be minimized with the proper training, forethought, caution, and equipment.

BE CONSIDERATE OF LANDOWNERS

Many put-ins, take-outs, and portages are open for public use. Others require that you cross private property. You will note that many landowners whose property borders popular canoeing rivers have posted their property against trespass. Paddlers can prevent additional closings by being thoughtful. Ask permission where it is possible; don't damage vegetation; park cars out of the way so they don't block roads; pick up litter. Make your portage expeditiously and leave; don't hang around picnicking and making a disturbance. Don't expect local residents to be responsible for rescuing you and your canoe. Dumping boats and getting them pinned on whitewater rivers happens to the best of us, and paddlers should prepare before launching by having suitable equipment, clothing, and a large enough group. Access to put-ins and take-outs is the right of a private landowner, and the privilege of the user. Access is becoming limited on some rivers, so it is increasingly important to maintain good relations with property owners.

USING THE RIVER GUIDE

Organization

Each chapter begins with a list of the rivers described. The tributaries of each river are indented and listed below it. The principal river is described first, then its tributaries in descending (downstream) order.

Format for River Descriptions

Each description starts with general information about the river as a whole. Longer rivers are then broken into sections that are of reasonable length for a canoe trip or which omit unrunnable sections of that river. These sections are introduced by a boldfaced heading and, in most cases, a table that summarizes significant information about that segment, such as what kind of water the paddler can expect; the recommended water level for paddling that section, and the season or conditions when that level is most likely to occur; what kind of scenery the river passes through; what maps to reference, directions and distances for portage; and total distances to be covered, in miles.

A new addition to the description is the date on which this information was verified by a volunteer river checker and that checker's initials. On rivers that have not recently been checked, it is recommended that paddlers investigate drops and other obstacles by scouting, if possible, before the section is run.

The tables codify the information that is usually required to plan trips rapidly. In the descriptive text that follows the tables, cumulative distances from the section starting point are placed within parentheses.

Table Format

Description:	(Difficulty of the river in this segment)
Date checked:	(Last date that information was verified as being correct, and initials of the person who verified it)
Navigable:	(Recommended water levels and seasons)
Scenery:	(What you will see from the boat)
Maps:	(US Geological Survey quadrangles and other maps)
Portages:	(Where to, when to, and how far to carry)

Starting Point-Ending Point   **Total miles**
Terminology: Difficulty of River

The following terms appear opposite the "Description" heading in the summary table and are used to describe the difficulty of the water to be paddled:

Lake The segment being described flows through a lake, or it is necessary to paddle across a lake to reach the beginning of a river.

Flatwater There is little or no current, and the river's surface is smooth and unbroken. Paddling upstream is easy.

Quickwater The river moves fast. Its surface is nearly smooth at high water levels, but is likely to be choppy at medium water levels and shallow at low water levels.

Marsh/swamp Vegetation often obstructs the river. Paddling may be slower than the distance alone would indicate.

Class Difficulty of rapids in a segment is rated according to American Whitewater Affiliation classifications: I, II, III, or IV.

See the appendix for a description of these classifications.

When two or more terms appear together opposite the "Description" heading in the summary table, the paddler should expect to encounter all of those conditions in that segment of the river. When one of these terms describes water conditions throughout most of the segment, it appears in boldface type.

Judging the difficulty of rapids is subjective. It depends on the type of boat, on how well paddlers read the river, and on how skillfully they maneuver their boats.

The difficulty of rapids changes with the water level. A given stretch of rapids may become easier or harder when there is more water in the river. Water level affects different parts of the same river differently. As a general rule, more water washes out a river with low gradient and small rocks, but it generates larger waves and more turbulence in a river that drops steeply through large rocks.

As water level rises, *current picks up*! Be aware of this. If the river is high and the air and water are cold, increase the rating by at least one—and possibly two—classes.

On small rivers, fallen trees present a greater hazard to paddlers than do rapids, especially since their location cannot be documented in advance. In rural areas, barbed wire fences frequently cross rivers and are hard to spot. Be alert and have your boat under control.

Terminology: Water Levels

The following terms appear opposite the "Navigable" heading in the summary tables. They describe the water level recommended for paddling a particular segment. The dates and conditions most likely to produce the recommended water level follow in parentheses.

Low water There is a clearly defined shoreline below the bank. Small rocky rivers will be uncanoeable, but flatter stretches and rapids in large rivers will be navigable.

Medium water The river extends to the bank, and soft vegetation along the shore may be under water. Marshy areas may be wet. Larger whitewater rivers, depending on the type of rapids, will be navigable at this water level, and dodging rocks will be the major entertainment.

High water The river is near the top of its defined bank, and alders along the shore may be under water. This is an acceptable water level for small whitewater rivers.

Very high water Large trees or clumps of smaller ones have their roots in the water. Reaching shore may be difficult or impossible. This water level is only recommended for experts who are familiar with the particular river and its problems.

Flood The river overflows its bank and makes pillows on large trees. This stage is dangerous for everyone.

Levels lower than those recommended do not necessarily mean that the river is not runnable; a river for which high water is recommended may be traveled in medium water, but it is likely to be scratchy, and paddlers may have to wade down some sections.

Terminology: Scenery

The following terms are used in the tables to describe the territory through which the river flows.

Wild Long sections of semiwilderness, with no more than a few isolated camps and occasional road access. Dirt roads may parallel the river within sight or sound, but only for short distances, and they do not noticeably alter the semiwilderness atmosphere of the trip. These roads may in fact be closed to the public or altogether impassable.

Forested Banks on both sides of the river look densely wooded, but there are good dirt and asphalt roads that follow along the river or are not far from it. These roads may frequently approach or cross the river. There may be farms and houses nearby, but not many of them are visible from the water.

Rural Farms are visible from the river, and some fields may extend down to the water.

Towns Small and isolated towns border the river. Aside from their effects on water quality, these towns have little impact on the trip.

Settled There are many houses or small buildings within sight or sound of the river.

Urban Multi-storied buildings are visible. The shorelines are frequently unattractive.

Maps

Each chart includes pertinent topographic maps in $7^1/_2$-minute series unless followed by "15" to indicate that they are in the 15-minute series. Topographic maps may be ordered from:

> Branch of Distribution, Eastern Region
> U.S. Geological Survey
> 1200 S. Eads Street
> Arlington, VA 22202

Portages

The portages in each chart are unavoidable carries, like those at dams and waterfalls, and difficult sections that usually are not runnable because of insufficient water. In addition, some rapids are listed as portages if they are significantly more difficult than the rating for that portion of the river. Unlisted portages included lift-overs to pass fallen trees and low, temporary bridges. There may also be additional carries around rapids that you do not wish to run. Portages that appear within parentheses are at the end of the river segment being described; only those who plan to paddle farther down the river need complete these portages.

Abbreviations

The following abbreviations are used in the summary tables:

ft   foot, feet
mi   mile, miles
yd   yard, yards
L   left
R   right
e   either
USGS   United States Geological Survey

Example: How to Read a Summary Table

Smithville-Brownville   3³/₄ mi

Description:	Class I-**II**
Date checked:	1990, JS
Navigable:	High water (April to early May)
Scenery:	Forested
Maps:	USGS Waitsfield
Portages:	1¹/₂ mi L **dam** 15 yd
	2 mi L **two ledges** 100 yd

Smithville-Brownville
   The starting point for this imaginary segment is Smithville. The
end point is Brownville.

3³/₄ mi
   The total distance to be covered is 3³/₄ miles.

Description: Class I-**II**
   Paddlers will encounter Class I and II whitewater on this segment.
Most of the segment is Class II.

Date checked: 1990, JS
   Jane Smith, a volunteer river checker, verified that the description
was accurate in 1990.

Navigable: High water (April to early May)
   The river is runnable at high water levels, which are most likely to
occur during April and the first part of May.

Scenery: Forested
   Paddlers will pass between wooded banks, but access roads may
exist in the woods, close to the river.

Map: USGS Waitsfield
   The topographic map for this segment is the US Geological
Survey Waitsfield 7¹/₂-minute quadrangle.

Portages: 1¹/₂ mi   L   **dam** 15 yd
              2 mi   L   **two ledges** 100 yd
   Paddlers will have to carry their boats for about 15 yards around a
dam about 1¹/₂ miles from Smithfield. The best route for the
portage is on the left as you face downstream. There is another
portage in ¹/₂ mile, 2 miles from the starting point at Smithville. The
best route is also on the left, and paddlers will have to carry their
boats about 100 yards to avoid two ledges. The last portage is not the
take-out point for the end of this section, however. If it were, it

would appear in parentheses to indicate that only those wanting to continue downriver need to complete that portage.

SECURITY

Regrettably, crime has reached canoeing rivers. At put-ins for some popular rivers, close to 100 percent of the parked cars are burglarized. To discourage this, do not leave money, cameras, or other valuables in cars. The first place thieves look is in your bag of dry clothes; leave your wallet at home. Take only the cash and cards that you will need, and carry them in a waterproof folder in your pocket. If this is not possible (for example, on an extended trip), pay to park your car at a gas station or at a house.

TIME

It's impossible to estimate time realistically for a canoe trip. Too many factors influence how long it will take: the water height, which affects the speed of the current; whether the boater pursues paddling as an athletic endeavor or prefers to float silently with the current, observing. A small, well-qualified party may scout nothing, while an instruction trip may scout everything. Paddlers may spend time bailing out canoes, taking pictures, or negotiating blowdowns.

On a large river with the current and wind favorably behind, the miles whiz by. On a small stream blocked with alder thickets and fallen trees, a paddler may take hours to travel a single mile. The same mile will require far less time when it is free of obstructions. It is good practice to select beforehand alternate end points for a trip, especially on an unfamiliar river.

RIVER LEVELS IN NEW ENGLAND

The water-level information given in the summary tables for individual rivers includes approximate dates, which are subject to wide variation from year to year. Some of the factors that influence water levels are discussed here.

Snow depth, temperature, rainfall, and transpiration are four seasonal factors that affect river levels. The farther south you go in New England, the less important the first two become, because there is usually less—or no—snow. As the snow cover disappears, temperature becomes less important, although runoff is greater and swifter when the ground is frozen. Once the leaves are out, surface runoff decreases substantially, because plants of all sizes use a great deal of water. Conversely, the fall foliage season invariably signals a rise in water levels. Significant rainfall is also more likely in autumn than it is in summer.

Terrain also must be considered. A river flowing from steep-sided hills and mountains will quickly collect the runoff from rainfall and melting snow. On the other hand, lakes, swamps, and gently rolling hills buffer the spring runoff, and the result is an extended canoeing season in spite of the weather. Knowledge of New England's topography will be as helpful to you as familiarity with its weather.

You must also take into account the nature of the river itself. If a river is flat, weather matters little as far as canoeability is concerned. If the river is steep and full of rapids, then heavy snow, warm temperatures, and moderate rainfall may all be necessary to keep it runnable. Also, you must consider the size of the river: a large river will generally peak and ebb more gradually, so it will have a much longer season than will a small stream.

Many of New England's rivers have just enough quickwater and easy rapids to make high or medium water necessary for good passage. In early March, rivers all over central and southern New England become runnable. Farther north, access to the water in early spring is hindered, first by snow and later by mud. Furthermore, ice shelves along the banks are hazardous in rapids and inconvenient elsewhere.

If you wish to run rapids in early March, Connecticut is the place. By late March the season in that state for good Class II and Class III rapids is fading, and you will probably be limited to some of the larger rivers. By May the rivers of northern New England, which are fed by melting snow deposits in the high mountains, are usually at optimal levels. Sometimes they are passable through Memorial Day, but there have been years when the season is over late in April.

Many of New England's rivers have gauges that have been set up by the US Geological Survey. Through a network known as the Telemark System, USGS district offices collect daily gauge readings for some of these rivers. This book contains occasional references to these gauges and other water level indicators, but comprehensive and detailed information about their use is not included.

River levels can vary tremendously from season to season, and unusually heavy rainfall can make any river passable at any time. If you do enough canoeing and kayaking, you will probably eventually meet someone who will defend winter boating, claiming that the canoeing season includes any sunny day when the temperature is above freezing.

Over a period of several years, a person who runs a lot of rivers develops a sense of river levels. Just as those who fish the ocean acquire an instinct for the tides, and those who live off the land can almost smell the weather, so it is with river people. After a while they get to know when a river runs and when it does not.

WATER RELEASES

With many of New England's rivers passable for only a few weeks in the spring or after an unusually heavy rainfall, releases of water from dams can extend the canoeing season in some localities. There are many dams on large New England rivers, but unless there are rapids below them, as is the case with the examples given, effects of releases may not be too noticeable.

The first type of release comes from dams used in connection with power generation. The Bear Swamp section of the Deerfield offers this type of release, providing Class II water.

The second type of release, often coordinated with paddling clubs, is the annual drawdown of lakes that are primarily used for summer recreation. The drawdown of Otis Reservoir, for example, offers two weekends of Class III-IV paddling every October on the upper Farmington.

The third type of release provides minimum flows in a river, for such diverse uses as power generation or sewage dilution. Tariffville Gorge on the Farmington benefits from this type of constant release.

The final type of release, just now being explored in the area, stems from the re-licensing of hydroelectric plants. The Monroe Bridge section of the Deerfield may benefit from this type of release in the future.

RENTALS

There are many places to rent canoes in New England, and they are easy to find. Begin your search in the Yellow Pages under "Canoes." Grumman and Old Town dealers may be able to help you locate distant outfitters. If not, you can obtain a copy of the Rent-a-Canoe Directory by writing to Grumman Boats, Marathon, NY 13803. The Mad River Canoe Company (Box 363, Waitsfield, VT 05673) and the Old Town Canoe Company (Old Town, ME 04468) can also supply you with smaller lists of dealers who rent their canoes.

RIVERS OMITTED FROM THIS GUIDE

Paddlers who would like to run a river that is not included in this guide and who are willing to report their findings may send a self-addressed stamped envelope to the AMC River Guide Committee (5 Joy St., Boston, MA 02108) to receive whatever information is available on that river.

Suggested Rivers with Flatwater and Quickwater Canoeing

Chapter	Page		State	Miles	Portages	Lake	Flatwater	Quickwater	Class I	Passable at all levels
8	211	**Concord River** (Concord—North Billerica)	MA	10¾			•			•
4	100	**Farmington River** (Farmington—Simsbury)	CT	13½			•			•
1	31	**Hammonasset River** (Green Hill Road—US 1)	CT	5¾			•			•
7	188	**Plum River**	MA	8			•			•
6	167	**Bass River**	MA	7			•			•
6	147	**Wood River** (RI 165—Alton)	RI	13¼	4	•	•	•	•	•
5	128	**Willimantic River** (Stafford Springs—Eagleville)	CT	14¾		•	•	•		

Suggested Rivers with Easy Rapids

Chapter	Page		State	Miles	Portages	Short Rapids	Long Rapids	Continuous Rapids	Flatwater	Quickwater	Class I	Class II	Class III
4	102	**Farmington River** (Hogback Dam—Collinsville)	CT	15¼		•	•		•	•	•		1
3	43	**Housatonic River** (Fall's Village—Kent)	CT	22½		•		•	•	•	•		1
4	116	**Salmon River System** (above covered bridge)	CT	5¼			•				•		
3	50	**Bantam River** (Bantam—Shepaug River)	CT	4¾		•				•			
4	70	**Deerfield River** (Bear Swamp—MA 2A)	MA	8½	1	•	•			•	•	1	
5	129	**Natchaug River** (CT 198—North Windham)	CT	2¾		•	•				•		
4	93	**Westfield River, North Branch**[1] (Cummington—West Chesterfield)	MA	7½		•	•				•		
4	97	**Westfield River, Middle Branch** (Smith's Hollow—Dayville)	MA	10		•	•				•	1	

[1] below 2.0 on MA–9 gauge

Suggested Rivers with Class III Rapids

Chapter	Page		State	Miles	Portages	Short Rapids	Long Rapids	Continuous Rapids	Class IV
4	64	**Millers River** (South Royalston—Athol)	MA	6¾			•		
4	96	**Westfield River, North Branch** (Knightsville Dam—Huntington)	MA	5		•			
4	105	**Farmington River** (Tarriffville Gorge)	CT	1½		•			
4	100	**Farmington River**[1] (New Boston section)	MA	3			•	•	
4	88	**Quaboag River**[2]	MA	5¼	1	•			1

[1] below 4.5 on gauge
[2] below 5.0 on gauge

Suggested Rivers with Class IV and V Rapids

Chapter	Page		State	Miles	Portages	Short Rapids	Long Rapids	Continuous Rapids	Class V
4	76	**Cold River** (MA 2—Deerfield River)	MA	4½	1		•	•	1
4	98	**Westfield River, West Branch** (Becket—Chester)	MA	9½	1		•	•	
3	43	**Housatonic River** (Bull's Bridge section)	CT	3¼		•			1
4	107	**Sandy Brook**	CT	4			•	•	
5	130	**Natchaug River** (Diana's Pool section)	CT	1		•			
4	74	**Deerfield River, West Branch**	VT	3	1		•	•	•
4	69	**Deerfield River** (Monroe Bridge section)	CT	4			•	•	

[1]above 10 on gauge

Chapter 1

Connecticut Coastal Watersheds

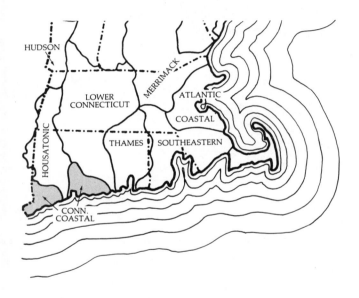

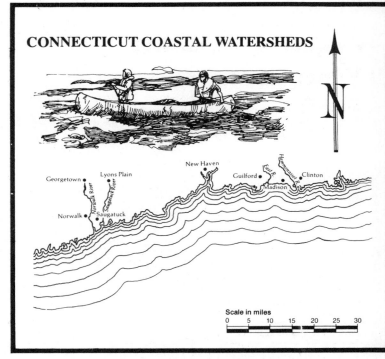

CONNECTICUT COASTAL WATERSHEDS

Georgetown •   Lyons Plain •   New Haven   Guilford •   Clinton

Norwalk •   Saugatuck   Madison

Norwalk River   Saugatuck River   East R.   Hammonasset R.

Scale in miles
0   5   10   15   20   25   30

 Three major rivers reach the sea in Connecticut: the Housatonic, the Connecticut, and the Thames. These and their tributaries drain a major portion of the interior, leaving little area to be drained by the coastal rivers. Thus the latter tend to be short, although several of them have nice tidal sections.

 Tidal streams are of particular interest for their flora and wildlife, which are more visible there than in most places, especially if you are alone and moving quietly. But it is necessary to watch the tide so as not to be caught on mudflats as the tide goes out.

 Two of the best rivers on the Connecticut coast are the East and Hammonasset.

NORWALK RIVER   CT

The Norwalk River is paralleled by US 7 and flows into Long Island Sound at Norwalk. In spite of its length, it is small and shallow, and it can only be run when there is a heavy runoff. A fair amount of the upper river is enjoyable, but not necessarily scenic. Much of the lower section through Norwalk is unattractive. See the USGS Norwalk North sheet.

One suggested 7-mile run begins at Old Mill Road about a mile below Georgetown. From there to the bridge in Cannondale it is Class I and occasionally blocked by debris. From Cannondale to the take-out just a few yards south of the Norwalk-Wilton line, the difficulty reaches Class II; there are only a few carries.

Below the Norwalk-Wilton line the rapids are considerably more difficult.

SAUGATUCK RIVER   CT

Maps: USGS Westport, Sherwood Point

The Saugatuck River flows south into Long Island Sound at Saugatuck in Westport. It is best to canoe the river early in the year, in March and early April.

Lyons Plain—Saugatuck   9 mi

Put in at Lyons Plain in Weston. It is a pleasant, 7-mile paddle with easy current through woodlands to tidewater, $1/2$ mile above Westport. There are a few small dams with short carries. Either take out at the bridge at tidewater, continue another $1/2$ mile to Westport, or continue an additional $1 1/2$ miles to Saugatuck, where you can take out near US 1. There are no good take-out spots near the mouth of the river.

EAST RIVER   CT

Nut Plains Road—Long Island Sound   6 mi

Description:	Tidal
Date checked:	1989, WB
Scenery:	Forested, rural
Map:	USGS Guilford

This river, which forms a part of the boundary between Guilford and Madison, is one of the nicest tidal streams along the Connecticut coast. It provides a pleasant and easy 6-mile paddle as it flows through woods to farmland, past some houses, and then out into the salt marshes. The houses are attractive, some are very old, and none is obtrusive. Most of the salt marsh is owned and preserved by the state or the Audubon Society.

Access upstream is from the upper end of Nut Plains Road, which is east of CT 77 and north of the Connecticut Turnpike (I-95). Near the ocean there is access at the US 1 bridge, the Guilford Town Dock, and the state launching ramp at the end of Neck Road in Madison.

HAMMONASSET RIVER   CT

The Hammonasset River runs south into Long Island Sound between Clinton and Madison. It is a pretty stream, and the Madison Land Trust has been acquiring land along the upper part in order to protect it. Unfortunately, filling and dredging at US 1 have ruined many acres of salt marsh, but there are still long stretches to the north and south of the highway where none of this is visible.

If you plan to paddle in the tidal portion immediately below the old fish hatchery, plan your trip for midtide or higher, or be ready to carry and drag over some rocks where the stream is too shallow. Tides run about a half hour earlier than Boston.

Off CT 79—US 1   7¹/₄ mi

Description:	**Flatwater, quickwater**, Class I-II; tidal
Date checked:	1989, WB
Navigable:	High water: needed above Green Hill Rd, early March
	Medium water: passable below Green Hill Rd, spring and fall
Scenery:	Forested, settled
Maps:	USGS Clinton

Follow Chestnut Hill Road northeast from CT 79 in Madison. Just before the bridge, turn north up Summer Hill Road and put in where it follows along the river.

At first the river drops gradually in easy Class II rapids. Just around the bend below Chestnut Hill Road, there is a footbridge, which can be passed on the right if the water is too high for you to pass under it. After about ¹/₂ mile of rapids, the stream runs for a while through a swamp and then into a pool above a broken, runnable dam. Green Hill Road is about 100 yards farther.

Below Green Hill Road (1¹/₂ mi) there is a long stretch that is flat, deep, and meandering. A broken, washed-out dam by the Connecticut Turnpike I-95)—at the site of an old fish hatchery—marks the beginning of tidewater.

Salt marshes begin at a bridge just above the Connecticut Turnpike (5¹/₂ mi) next to exit 62, where there is a road on the left. Paddle through salt marshes the rest of the way to US 1 (7¹/₄ mi). In another mile the river opens into Clinton Harbor (8¹/₄ mi).

Chapter 2

Hudson Watershed

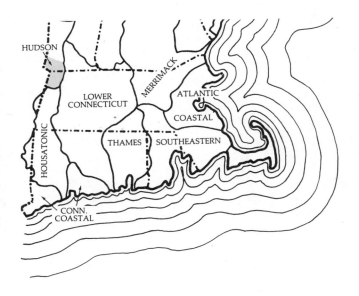

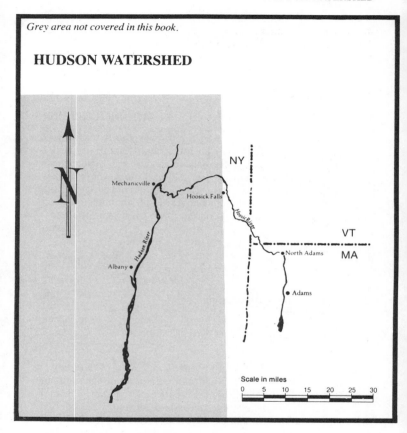

Grey area not covered in this book.

HUDSON WATERSHED

The water that falls in western Massachusetts and Connecticut is forced eastward by the Taconic Mountains, which lie along the New York state line. Almost all of it subsequently finds its way into the Housatonic River and thence southward into Long Island Sound. A *small portion of the drainage in the northwest corner of Massachusetts wanders northwestward, making a breach in the range demarking the Taconic and Green mountains. The Hoosic River crosses the southwest corner of Vermont and continues its northwestern course to the Hudson River.*

HOOSIC RIVER   MA, VT, NY

The Hoosic River rises in Lanesboro, Massachusetts, flows north to North Adams, turns west to Williamstown, and then takes off northwesterly across a corner of Vermont into New York, where it again turns north to make a big loop to meet the Hudson River near Mechanicsville. The flood-control works in Adams and North Adams have reduced the pollution from the mills there, but it is still far from the beautiful stream that the Mohawks possessed in early days.

The flood-control works have also eliminated the canoeing in Adams and North Adams, as the river drops sharply between high retaining walls. Boating is not only suicidal there, it is illegal.

The upper sections are only passable in high water, but below North Adams much of it can be done later in the year.

Cheshire Reservoir—First Adams Dam   4¹/₂ mi

Description:	Quickwater, swamp
Date checked:	1985
Navigable:	Medium or high water
Scenery:	Swamp, forested, towns
Maps:	USGS Cheshire, Windsor
Portage:	(4¹/₂ mi e dam 100 yd)

Put in from MA 8 at the outlet of the Cheshire Reservoir. The stream is small, open, and fast for the first mile to the first bridge. Then it starts to diffuse into a wider area, meandering back and forth, coming into a small open area by a farm and passing under a small bridge before coming to a dam.

This bridge is reached by turning east from MA 8 on to the first (obscure) road downstream of East View Drive.

First Adams Dam—MA 8 Bridge   1 mi

Description:	Class II
Date checked:	1985
Navigable:	Medium to high water
Scenery:	Town
Map:	USGS North Adams

This run is delightful, albeit short. Take out at the park at the low bridge immediately downstream of the high MA 8 bridge.

Through Adams   3 mi

Below the next MA 8 bridge (¹/₂ mi), the river starts a steeper drop to the channelization for flood control, which extends through Adams. Canoeing in this area is both dangerous and illegal, as the river drops over dams confined within vertical cement retaining walls.

Adams—North Adams   4 mi

Description:	Quickwater
Date checked:	1985
Navigable:	Medium to high water
Scenery:	Town
Map:	USGS North Adams

Put in at the Lime Street bridge at the north end of Adams, at the end of the dikes. The river size is augmented slightly here, and the water quality has deteriorated. This section is also prone to extensive log jams.

Take out at the MA 8A bridge (3 mi) or with difficulty a mile farther at the start of the dikes.

Through North Adams 4¹/₂ mi

The flood channelization starts well south of North Adams and continues all the way through town and on to the west. Portage by car.

North Adams—North Pownal, VT 11³/₄ mi

Description:	**Quickwater,** Class I, **II**
Date checked:	1985
Navigable:	Medium water
Scenery:	Towns, rural, forested
Maps:	USGS North Adams, Williamstown, MA; North Pownal, VT
Portage:	11¹/₄ mi R dam in North Pownal ¹/₄ mi)

Put in below the last dam at the west end of North Adams, just west of the Protection Road bridge. The most convenient place is the old sewage treatment plant on the north side.

Most of the distance is smooth, with only an occasional rapid of moderate difficulty, spaced with stretches of quieter water between them. Two bridges close together are passed in a little more than a mile. You then encounter the bridge that carries the Appalachian Trail (3 mi), the US 7 bridge in Williamstown (4¹/₄ mi), and the Massachusetts-Vermont line (6¹/₄ mi). The bridge at Pownal crosses at 9 miles.

The dam at North Pownal is confined between cliffs and walls, so it should be scouted in advance. Carry up the road on either side, although neither is easy. By the time the factory chimney can be seen from the river you may be past the best take-out.

Chapter 3

Housatonic Watershed

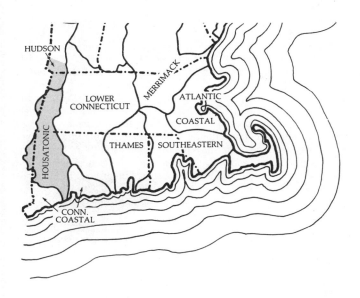

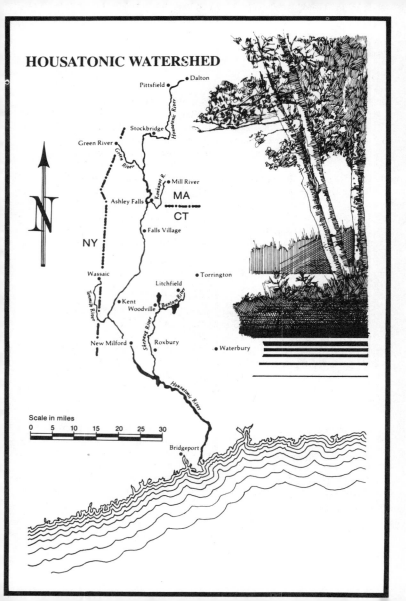

HOUSATONIC WATERSHED

Dalton

Pittsfield

Stockbridge

Housatonic River

Green River

Green River

Mill River

Konkapot R.

Ashley Falls

MA

CT

NY

Falls Village

N

Wassaic

Torrington

Litchfield

Bantam River

Kent

Woodville

Tenmile River

Shepaug River

New Milford

Roxbury

Waterbury

Housatonic River

Scale in miles

0   5   10   15   20   25   30

Bridgeport

HOUSATONIC RIVER   MA, CT

Maps:	USGS Pittsfield East, Pittsfield West, East Lee, Stockbridge, Great Barrington, Ashley Falls, South Canaan, Cornwall, Ellsworth, Kent, Dover Plains, New Milford, Danbury, Newtown, Southbury, Long Hill, Ansonia, Milford

The Housatonic River rises near Pittsfield, Massachusetts, flows south through the wide valley between the Berkshire Hills on the east and the Taconic Range on the west, and continues through Connecticut to reach the sea between Stratford and Milford. It is called by its Indian name, which means "river beyond the mountains." Its total length from Hinsdale, Massachusetts, to the sea is 142 miles.

Dalton—Lenox   19 mi

Put in below the last dam in Dalton. The river is somewhat polluted by the paper mills there and again at Pittsfield by the Pittsfield sewage plant, so this section is not particularly recommended. Below Dalton, and all the way to Lenox, it is mostly a flat, winding river, but there are stimulating views of Greylock from the meandering stream. This section is best canoed in the spring when the water is high, the current fast, and the pollution at a minimum.

Lenox—Stockbridge   12 mi

Just below Lenox ($^1/_2$ mile) is a dam and, again at Lee ($1^1/_2$ miles), there are two more dams. This part is flat with some rapids. From here to Stockbridge the river is wilder and more attractive, as the stream winds through a swampy, overgrown section with some small rips.

Stockbridge—Great Barrington   13 mi

The first few miles through the Stockbridge meadows to Glendale are very winding, but at high water there is a fast current. There are two dams below Glendale with a bad rapid below the second. The river then widens into a lake for $1^1/2$ miles to another dam. Just above Housatonic is a dam with a bad rapid below, then 1 mile of lake to the dam at Risingdale. The remaining 5 miles to the dam in Great Barrington are flatwater, with the Williams River entering from the right 1 mile down.

Great Barrington—Falls Village   25 mi

Description:	**Flatwater,** quickwater, Class I, II
Date checked:	1985
Navigable:	Passable at all water levels
Scenery:	Wild, forested, rural
Maps:	USGS Great Barrington, Ashley Falls, South Canaan
Portages:	19 mi; island dam W of Canaan
	24 mi; L dam above Falls Village 160 yd

This stretch is mostly flatwater with only two dams. From the dam in Great Barrington it is 2 miles to the mouth of the Green River, which enters on the right. The Konkapot River enters on the left at Ashley Falls, just above the Connecticut line (17 miles). Another 2 miles brings one to the old dam west of Canaan and, 5 miles later, to the dam (24 miles) above Falls Village. Use extreme caution when running this section, due to old reinforcing rods under surface. The safest run is far left. There was a gristmill at Falls Village as early as 1740. Here in 1744 was built the first bridge in this section across the Housatonic, later known as Burral's Bridge.

Falls Village—Kent (Bull's Bridge) 27$^1/_2$ mi

Description:	**Quickwater,** Class **I, II,** III, IV
Date checked:	1989, WC, ST
Navigable:	Dam controlled
Scenery:	Forested, rural, towns, settled
Maps:	USGS South Canaan, Cornwall, Ellsworth, Kent, Dover Plains

Mention should be made of the Class III-IV rapid above Falls Village, just below the Great Falls. To run it, put in from the left. Rattlesnake Rapid twists through granite ledges and ends with an 8-foot plunge just above the bridge. A slalom course has been set up in this area.

The river below the hydroelectric station in Falls Village is a favorite one-day trip with much smoothwater, alternating with Class I and II water, and a more difficult rapid at the covered bridge in West Cornwall.

The water level is controlled at the powerhouse at Falls Village. Most put in at a rest area across from the powerhouse. There is a tricky corner just below, which novices should scout before starting. There are no particular problems, except for many small rips that can be dangerous in high water, until West Cornwall is reached 7$^1/_2$ miles downstream. **Caution!** There is a long wooden bridge here, and one should pull out well above it to look over the $^1/_4$ mile of rapids (Class II-III) which starts just above the bridge and runs down to the corner below. This can be dangerous (Class IV) at high water. For some miles below this point, the river runs beside Housatonic Meadows State Park. The next 9 miles to Kent are mostly quickwater except for a drop over a ledge about 1 mile below Cornwall Bridge, at the former site of Swift's Bridge. The remaining 5 miles to the dam at Bull's Bridge are flatwater. Most day trippers from Fall's Village take out above the CT 341 bridge on a dirt road on the right side of the river.

Bull's Bridge—Gaylordsville   3¹/₄ mi

Description:	Class **IV**, V
Date checked:	1989, JM
Navigable:	High and medium water: March, April
	Low water: Summer releases
Scenery:	Forested
Map:	USGS Kent

This section is the biggest water described in this *Guide*. Put in at the covered bridge. For a Class V start, carry up above the bridge to the tip of the island. The Staircase is the drop on the left, and should be carefully scouted. The bottom is riddled with potholes. Several essential moves must be made in quick succession.

For a Class IV run, put in below the bridge. The Funnel lies immediately downstream. The Funnel must be run on the right, but the water coming from the right side of the island pushes you left. The drop ¹/₂ mile below should be scouted from the left. There is a nasty hole on the right. The rapids get slightly easier after the Ten Mile River enters from the right. The Appalachian Trail crosses the Ten Mile at this point on a footbridge. There are two more heavy rapids to the take-out, but they are not as difficult as those above. These two rapids are often run in conjunction with a trip on the Ten Mile. It is also possible to put in below the Funnel by following the Appalachian Trail downstream on the right bank. Take out at the US 7 bridge in Gaylordsville.

Gaylordsville—Long Island Sound   45 mi

Description:	Quickwater, **flatwater,** tidal
Date checked:	1985
Navigable:	Navigable at all water levels
Scenery:	Forested, rural, towns, urban
Maps:	USGS New Milford, Danbury, Newtown,
	Southbury, Long Hill, Ansonia, Milford
Portages:	10 mi dam at New Milford
	20 mi Shepaug Dam
	28 mi Stevenson Dam
	33 mi Shelton Dam

None of these portages is recommended. It is suggested that the lakes between the dams be done as separate trips. The 10 miles to the dam at New Milford is mostly strong current. The Shepaug Dam backs the river nearly to New Milford; the Stevenson Dam backs the river nearly to the Shepaug Dam; the Shelton Dam backs water nearly to the Stevenson Dam. The remainder of the river is tidal.

GREEN RIVER   NY, MA

Maps: USGS State Line, Egremont, Great Barrington

The Green River rises in Austerlitz, New York, and flows southeastward to enter the Housatonic just below Great Barrington. It is a beautiful, clear, limestone brook with NY 71 following it most of the way. It is small and must be canoed during freshet or after heavy rains.

Green River—Housatonic River   12 mi

A start can be made at Green River village, but the first 1 1/2 miles to a bridge on the side road off NY 71 are extremely rough. The going then becomes easier for 2 miles to the NY 71 bridge. This section is all quickwater with numerous short rapids and some very shallow places. The valley is all open farmland along here. The New York-Massachusetts border is crossed and then it is only 2 miles to North Egremont, passing two bridges along the way. **Caution!** All through the lower part of this river watch for barbed wire. Pass through broad meadows and lift over occasional logs for the 2 miles from North Egremont to the Egremont Plains road bridge. The current continues strong for another 2 miles to the MA 23 bridge. The remaining 2 miles to the US 7 bridge, where the river joins the Housatonic River, are through broad meadows.

KONKAPOT RIVER   MA, CT

The Konkapot arises in Lake Buel in Monterey and flows south across the Connecticut line, where it turns west and north, recrossing into Massachusetts to flow into the Housatonic at Ashley Falls.

Mill River—Konkapot Road   4 mi

Description:	Class **II, III,** IV
Date checked:	1989, NH, AH
Navigable:	High water: March, April
Scenery:	Rural, settled
Maps:	USGS Great Barrington, Ashley Falls

This is a small, narrow whitewater stream that runs through a mixture of pastures and small towns. There are numerous small broken dams that could create hazards at higher water levels, but which, at lower levels, are Class II-III and do not require scouting if approached with caution.

Put in just below a mill dam in the hamlet of Mill River on Hayes Hill Road just off MA 57. One-half mile downstream is a washed-out dam, Class III at low levels, Class IV at high levels. Scout on the left. The best run is left center over an exposed ledge. No other scouting is required at low to medium levels. Take note of a scenic waterfall (Umpachene Falls) 1/4 mile below the second bridge for an enjoyable short hike and a good picnic spot.

Be aware of a fence stretched across the river 1/2 mile below the falls. It is not a problem at low to medium levels. Line boats on the left. Strainers may be present at any corner so be alert as you paddle.

There is an excellent take-out at a small sandy beach on the right just below the Konkapot Road bridge, off Southfield Road.

TEN MILE RIVER   NY, CT

The Ten Mile River rises in Salisbury, Connecticut, where it is known as Webatuck Creek. It flows southwest into New York, where just below Wassaic it is joined by Wassaic Creek and becomes known as the Ten Mile River. It then flows south and finally turns east to meet the Housatonic just below Bulls Bridge in Connecticut. Although it starts and ends in Connecticut, most of the running on the river is in New York. This river has a number of difficult rapids and should not be attempted by novices, especially at the lower end. It is best run during medium water stages, as at high water some pitches can be difficult, and at low water impassable.

Wassaic—Webatuck   **14 mi**

Maps:	USGS Amenia, Dover Plains

Put in about $^1/_2$ mile below Wassaic, near the bridge at the Wassaic State School. At high water one can put in a mile farther upstream near South Amenia. There are two difficult pitches just below the start, then fast, smooth current around sharp turns in the meadows for 5 miles to Dover Plains, where there is a dam that must be carried. Just below is a broken dam that can usually be run, followed by 8 miles of easy, pleasant running to the dam at South Dover. For the next 5 miles from here to the Housatonic, the stream is deeper and more sporting where it cuts through the hills. There are some rough turns 1 mile below the bridge at South Dover and again at Webatuck.

Webatuck—Housatonic River   **4 mi**

Description:	**Quickwater,** Class I, **II,** III, IV
Date checked:	1985
Navigable:	High water: spring
Scenery:	Forested, rural, settled
Map:	USGS Dover Plains

At the New York-Connecticut state line ($1^1/_2$ miles), there is a steep chute with waves and a tricky outrun. **Caution!** The waves are high here and the pitch should be looked over carefully before running. Below here the rapids are less difficult until the confluence with the Housatonic River, which is quite rocky and may be difficult in high water. There is no pause on entering that river, as the difficult rapids continue.

SHEPAUG RIVER   **CT**

The Shepaug is a popular early-season whitewater run. A water-supply reservoir in its headwaters means the upper section is rarely runnable. Below Roxbury Station, the recommended take-out, lies the unrunnable Roxbury Falls. There is no easily accessible take-out just above the falls because it is located in a narrow gorge. This is an extremely dangerous spot.

Woodville—Bee Brook (CT 47)   6 mi

Description:	Class II-III
Date checked:	1989, RW
Navigable:	High and medium water: March
Scenery:	Forested
Map:	USGS New Preston

To put in below the dam, take the first road upstream on the west side of the river (CT 341) from US 202, and then take the first right. Follow upstream and put in where the road approaches the river. Water levels are unpredictable and can rise rapidly after heavy rain or snow.

The first mile below the start is fast, twisty, and Class III. None of the drops requires scouting, but they can be quite narrow and technical. Watch for fallen trees. Several islands complicate the choice of routes. After the high US 202 bridge, there are two more miles with numerous, short Class III rapids, and one sharp drop that has numerous rocks, before the confluence with the Bantam River. The Shepaug flows through a narrow forested valley with large groves of hemlocks. Romford Road follows the Shepaug for most of the way, but it is often out of sight.

After the confluence with the Bantam (3 mi), the Shepaug's volume is much greater, and the river becomes less technical. Intermittent rapids continue, sometimes reaching Class III in difficulty, for 3 miles to the CT 47 bridge (6 mi), a mile above Washington Depot. This bridge is called Bee Brook for the small stream that enters on the right just upstream of the bridge.

Bee Brook (CT 47)—Roxbury Station   9¹/₂ mi

Description:	Class II
Date checked:	1989, RW
Navigable:	High and medium water: March
Scenery:	Forested
Maps:	USGS New Preston, Roxbury

The section from Washington Depot to Roxbury is one of the most attractive whitewater runs in Connecticut. Beautiful, steep, hemlock-covered banks rise 300 to 500 feet above the river; in a few places there are scenic cliffs. Evidence of civilization is minimal. The rapids are intermittent Class II, permitting easy running without the need for scouting.

Below the first CT 47 bridge (Bee Brook), the Shepaug is gentler than above. One-and-a-half miles of Class II rapids lead past two more CT 47 bridges in Washington Depot. Then there are 6 miles of scenic Class II rapids through the "clamshell" area, a deep canyon and a bend in the river away from all roads. The river flattens out for the next 2 miles to Roxbury Station. Take out at Hodge Park on CT 67 (9¹/₂ mi) where the road on the east bank is close to the river, ¹/₄ mile above a small roller dam.

Caution! Four miles below the dam at Roxbury Station is Roxbury Falls. It is a trap. The approach is blind, and many canoeists, caught in the swift current as they approached it, have been swept over it. The steep walls and strong current at the top make a safe landing and exit both difficult and unlikely. Below Roxbury Falls it is only a mile to the ponding in Lake Lillinoah.

BANTAM RIVER   CT

The Bantam River is a small stream that rises in Litchfield and joins the Shepaug in Washington. It is one of the early whitewater runs in New England—the first weekends of March bring many groups to the Bantam. Because of the river's small size, it is sometimes plagued by fallen trees and dangerous ice ledges.

Litchfield—Bantam   9¹/₄ mi

Put in at the CT 25 bridge northeast of Litchfield. The pretty, narrow stream winds slowly through swampland to Bantam Lake (5³/₄ mi). It is about ³/₄ mile along the north shore around a promontory to the outlet (6¹/₂ mi). It is then a little over 1¹/₂ miles to the town of Bantam, where there is a dam.

Paddlers can put in where the river turns sharply left in Bantam (8¹/₂ mi), but novice groups desiring whitewater would be better off further down. The first ³/₄ mile from Bantam to a bridge on Stoddard Road is Class III, with a high probability of tree obstructions.

Bantam—Shepaug River   4³/₄ mi

Description:	Class I-II
Date checked:	1988, ST
Navigable:	High water: March
Scenery:	Forested
Maps:	USGS West Torrington, Litchfield, New Preston
Portage:	2¹/₄ mi L broken dam at West Morris 30 yd (optional)

The best start for an easy whitewater trip is at the Stoddard Road bridge, reached by going south on West Morris Road from CT 25 in Bantam and following the former until Stoddard Road leaves on the left. There are easy Class II rapids for ¹/₂ mile to the next bridge and another 1³/₄ miles of similar rapids to a broken dam and a bridge in West Morris. This dam is occasionally run, but it should be looked over. It is generally carried.

Below West Morris (2¹/₄ mi) there are 2 miles of more difficult Class II rapids to the steel bridge at Rumsey Hall School (4¹/₄ mi). One-half mile more of rapids brings the boater to the confluence with the Shepaug River (4³/₄ mi). Take out either at Rumsey Hall School or at CT 47, which is 3 miles down the Shepaug.

Chapter 4

Lower Connecticut Watershed

LOWER CONNECTICUT WATERSHED

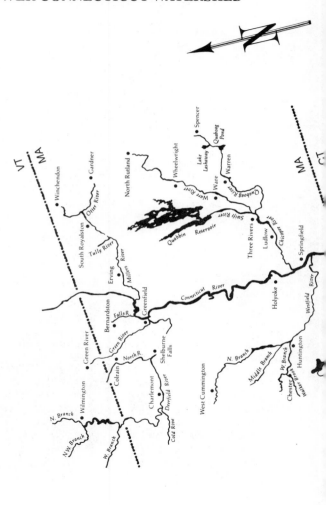

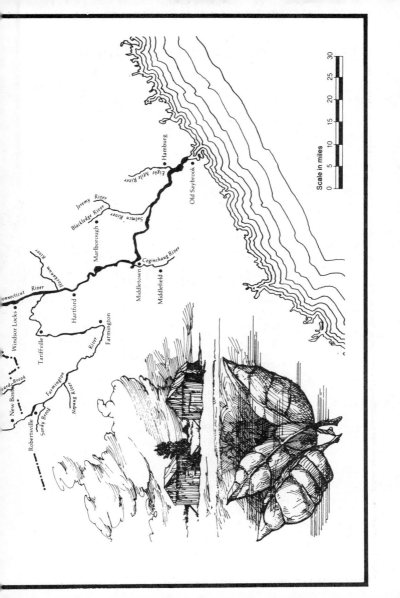

Scale in miles

0   5   10   15   20   25   30

Connecticut River
Windsor Locks
New Bos...
...ard Brook
Tariffville
Robertsville
Sandy Brook
Farmington River
Nepaug River
Farmington River
Farmington
Hartford
Housatonic River
Coginchaug River
Middletown
Middlefield
Marlborough
Blackledge River
Salmon River
Jeremy River
Eight Mile River
Hamburg
Old Saybrook

The Connecticut River dominates New Hampshire, Vermont, Massachusetts, and Connecticut, and it captures much of the water that falls in these states. It is already a large river when it crosses from New Hampshire into Massachusetts. Many of its best known and frequently canoed tributaries lie to the north. Only those tributaries whose confluence lie south of the New Hampshire-Vermont line are included in this volume of the River Guide. *An illustrated guidebook with maps of the Connecticut River is available from the Connecticut River Watershed Council, Inc., 125 Combs Road, Easthampton, MA 01027 (413-584-0057). A four-color navigation map of the Massachusetts section is available from New England Cartographics, P.O. Box 369, Amherst, MA 01004.*

CONNECTICUT RIVER   MA, CT

Vernon Dam—Turners Falls   21¹/₂ mi

Description:	**Flatwater,** quickwater, Class I-II
Date checked:	1989, CR
Navigable:	Navigable at all water levels
Scenery:	Forested, rural, settled
Maps:	USGS Brattleboro, Keene, Northfield, Millers Falls, Greenfield
Portage:	(21¹/₂ mi R Turners Falls Dam, west side of Barton Dam state ramp)
Campsites:	13 mi L Northeast Utilities, Munn's Ferry Campground
	19¹/₂ mi R Northeast Utilities, Barton Cove Campsite

Below the Vernon Dam the going is swift and may be rocky when the water is low. After a sharp turn, Stebbin Island is passed (1 mi). At 2 miles, the mouth of the Ashuelot River is met on the left in Hinsdale, New Hampshire. During periods of low water you can paddle upstream on the Ashuelot into Hinsdale to obtain supplies. Below the confluence with the Ashuelot, a small island, then a railroad bridge (3 mi) are passed. The Massachusetts border is crossed at $6^1/2$ miles, and the MA 142 (Schell Bridge) is reached at $8^1/2$ miles. Note the state-owned Pauchaug Brook public-access area on the left just above the bridge. The access ramp has a large, paved parking area. One-half mile farther another railroad bridge (9 mi) is reached. The river continues along flat water for some distance, but canoeists should exercise caution around power boats, which travel South on this stretch of the river to the Turners Falls Dam. Power-boat use diminishes greatly during the weekdays. The Munns Ferry Boat Camping Area is reached on the left bank at 13 miles. Northeast Utilities provides water, shelters, campsites, and firewood free of charge to the boating public on a first-come-first-served basis. The campsite fills quickly during summer weekends. About 1 mile from the campsite, Riverview Picnic Area can be seen on the left. At 16 miles the intake/outlet of the famous Northfield Mountain pumped-storage hydroelectric facility is reached. Do not paddle past the line of floating buoy markers. From there it is 5 miles to the French King Gorge, at the upper end of which is a large rock (17 mi) in the middle of the channel. French King Rock may cause turbulence even when the rest of the river is calm. A route close to either shore is preferred at this point. The current quickens as the river turns right after passing under the French King Bridge (MA 2), and the confluence with the Millers River on the left. At high water this section of the river can become extremely rough; under these conditions, some canoeists may prefer to take out at the bridge that crosses the Millers River at its mouth.

The current slackens after this section as the river enters the pool behind the Turners Falls Dam. Parts of the river here can be very deep. Eventually campsites can be seen on the right bank. Continuing, the river narrows and comes out onto Barton Cove (21 mi) and passes the tip of the peninsula that forms Barton Cove Campsite. The state boat ramp lies straight ahead, with Barton Island on the right. The campsite can be reached by going right after the peninsula's tip and keeping the island on the left. Canoeists may wish to explore the ancient, rocky plunge pools and their hidden lagoons along the west shore of the campground peninsula.

At Turners Falls one should take out at the public boat ramp on the west side of Barton Cove. Portage arrangements can be made by calling Northeast Utilities, Northfield Mountain Superintendent,

Northfield, MA (413-774-2221, x4451) at least three days in advance of your arrival. Call again when you reach the boat ramp.

The section of river below the dam requires a 3-mile portage through Turners Falls to the Montague City Bridge. There is very little water between these two points except during flood, when canoeing is not advised. Most of the water is diverted to the power canal, where canoeing is not allowed.

Turners Falls—Northampton   21¹/₂ mi

Description:	**Flatwater,** quickwater
Date checked:	1989, CR
Navigable:	Navigable at all water levels
Scenery:	Rural, forested, towns
Maps:	USGS Millers Falls, Greenfield, Mt. Toby, Mt. Holyoke, Easthampton
Campsites:	¹/₂ mi Cabot Island
	7 mi Second Island

The 3¹/₂ miles of river below the Turners Falls Dam to the Montague City Bridge cannot be run even by experienced canoeists. Most canoeists will, therefore, make the long carry to put in at the Montague City bridge 3¹/₂ miles below the dam, just below the confluence with the Deerfield River. Camping is possible a short distance upstream from the confluence along the Connecticut River on Cabot Island. The island is owned by, and sits opposite, Western Massachusetts Electric Company's Cabot Hydro Station. A nice side trip is possible upstream on the Deerfield River. Access points on the Deerfield are located at the MA 5 or US 91 bridges.

The next 21 miles to Northampton are easy paddling with little interference from power boats along most of the way. This section of the river is considered to be the most remote for canoeists. Although the way is through farmland, the 20-foot high riverbanks generally block the view of the fields. As most of these fields are cultivated down to the river bank, the best camping spots on this stretch are on the islands in the river. After passing a low, treeless island (1 mi) on the right, the B&M railroad bridge (2¹/₂ mi) is reached. Soon the confluence with the Saw Mill River appears on the left. Third Island, owned by the Connecticut River Watershed Council, is on the right at 4 miles. Mt. Toby is soon visible on the horizon. At the bend in the river, Cranberry Pond Brook enters on the left. If you land your canoe on the rocks at this point, a short side-hike up the steep bank will be rewarded with a view of a scenic waterfall. Turning west here, the river affords a fine view of Mt. Sugarloaf, and, at 7 miles, Second Island provides excellent primitive camping on town conservation land. It is another 3 miles to the MA 116 bridge in Sunderland. A public access on the left at 11 miles provides a small parking area. From here it is a very short walk into the village of Sunderland to obtain supplies. Across the river from this access is an unofficial access point where canoeists might tie down and enjoy a 1-mile side-hike on a blue-blazed trail to the summit of South Sugarloaf Mountain. The mountain affords a scenic, panoramic view of the Connecticut River valley.

For the next several miles the river runs through a wide valley. The setting is very rural and little can be seen of civilization. At 15 miles the river takes a sharp right turn, where sandstone ledges on the left bank make a good picnic spot. A sandy beach on the right offers a good camping place if the owner's permission is obtained. The next 4 miles form a large oxbow around the town of Hadley. Power boat activity increases at this point, but it generally does not pose a hazard. Where Cow Bridge Brook enters on the right (16 mi) there is a public access ramp. The river takes a straight course for the next 3 miles, passing the confluence of the Mill River on the left (17 mi). A small access area is located here. Once around Hadley, the river proceeds straight again, passing another Mill River on the right bank at 19 miles. The river takes a sharp U-turn left just after passing between Canary Island on the right and Scott Island on the left. Both islands are heavily used for camping by the power boaters, who are now quite numerous at this point in the river. A route close to either shore is advised during weekends. The north tip of Elwell Island (20$\frac{1}{2}$ mi) is reached as the U-turn is completed. The island is a popular camping spot for river users. A route along the channel on the right bank is preferred during busy days and offers total solitude for canoeists. After passing under an abandoned railroad bridge, the MA 9 bridge is reached. The Sportsman's Marina at the east end of the bridge offers a launching area and permits camping and car spotting for a small fee.

Northampton—Holyoke Dam   11 mi

Description:	**Flatwater,** quickwater
Date checked:	1989, CR
Navigable:	Navigable at all water levels
Scenery:	Rural, forested, settled, urban
Maps:	USGS Mt. Holyoke, Easthampton, Springfield North, Mt. Tom
Portage:	(11 mi L Holyoke Dam)
Campsites:	1/2 mi Sportsman's Marina
	2 mi Rainbow Beach

The river now makes a large bend around Northampton. Below the bridge is the old shepherd island (2 mi) that has now been connected to Rainbow Beach by natural river action. The entire area on the right bank is state owned and allows for suitable primitive camping. This section of river is perhaps the most beautiful, but it is also the most heavily traveled by power boats. A route close to either shore is advised, particularly on weekends. Mitch's Marina (3 mi) on the left bank offers a launching area and picnic tables. Just after the marina is a privately owned island in mid-channel. Below that island, on the right, is the Mill River (4 mi), the scene of the great flood of May 16, 1874, in which 141 lives were lost. Just below here is the entrance to the Oxbow that was created during the flood. One may paddle up this waterway 1 1/2 miles to Hulbert's Pond and the Arcadia Wildlife Sanctuary. The sanctuary hosts the headquarters of the Connecticut River Watershed Council. Oxbow Marina is located 1/2 mile farther on the Oxbow. From the Oxbow entrance the river turns eastward for 1 mile and cuts through the Holyoke Range, with Mt. Nonotuck and Mt. Tom on the right and Mt. Holyoke on the left. At 5 miles the Mt. Tom power station is passed on the right and the scenic high cliffs of Titan's Pier are on the left. Bachelor Brook enters on the left at 6 1/2 miles and Stoney Brook at 7 miles. Brunnelle's Marina on the left offers an opportunity for a vehicle portage around the Holyoke Dam, which is located 4 miles downstream. Call the Holyoke Water Power Company (413-536-9441 during business hours, 536-9458 or 9449 at other times). You should call at least three days in advance of your planned arrival, then call again when you reach the marina. If you prefer to self-portage, you may continue downstream to the dam. It is about $1/2$ mile to the famous Dinosaur Tracks just above the ledges where MA 5 comes close to the river on the right. Continuing, the river narrows as it passes through a rocky gorge where the water can be rough at times. As you near the dam, pull out on the left bank at the southern end of a peninsula about 200 yards above the US 202 bridge. Ascend the steep 20-foot bank to Canal Street and walk $1/4$ mile past the MA 116 bridge. Put in just beyond a playground under the bridge on an unpaved public access.

Holyoke Dam—Enfield Dam $18^1/2$ mi

Description:	**Flatwater,** quickwater
Date checked:	1989, CR
Navigable:	Navigable at all water levels
Scenery:	Rural, forested, settled, urban
Maps:	USGS Springfield North, Mt. Tom, Springfield South, Broad Brook
Portage:	($18^1/2$ mi R Enfield Dam)

At the dam, the river is shallow and quite swift. In 2 miles the B&M railroad and MA 141/116 bridges are passed. This is a heavily populated area with unattractive riverbanks, but, as Holyoke is left behind, the landscape improves. There is a paved public access and parking area on the left just below the Massachusetts Turnpike Bridge ($5^1/2$ mi). At 6 miles the Chicopee River enters on the left. The North End Bridge is reached at 9 miles and, just below, Bassett's Marina on the left offers a good launching spot. Soon the Conrail and the Memorial bridges are passed and Riverfront Park becomes visible on the left. The Bondi's Island Boat Ramp is soon reached on the right bank. After passing the Westfield River on the right in $1/2$ mile, one reaches the South End Bridge. Here the Agawam Yacht

Club offers access on the right bank. From this point the river flows southward with low banks through a mostly rural setting. A lengthy sandbar on the left bank indicates the location of the Stebbin Wildlife Refuge, which extends about 3 miles to the Massachusetts-Connecticut boundary. Two miles below the border is the dismantled CT 190 bridge at Thompsonville. There is a town boat ramp just below the bridge abutments on the left bank. From here it is only 3/4 mile, mostly through tobacco fields, to the new CT 190 bridge and the Enfield Dam. On the right bank is a state boat ramp in Suffield. Take out here to portage the dam, which is immediately below the bridge. The dam crosses diagonally, slanting downstream toward the right bank. This 9-foot-high dam has been breached in several locations. Although it has been shot by experienced canoeists at low water, it is not recommended.

Enfield Dam—Wethersfield Cove   20 mi

Description:	**Flatwater,** quickwater, Class I
Date checked:	1985
Navigable:	Passable at all water levels
Scenery:	Rural, forested, settled, urban
Maps:	USGS Broad Brook, Manchester, Hartford North, Hartford South

One can lift over the dam and run the 4 1/2 miles of easy rapids through rough wooded country to the canal outlet opposite Windsor Locks. Most canoeists, however, use the canal.

Land on the west shore just above the lock, lift the canoe into the canal, and paddle down to the lower lock, which should not be approached too closely because of the currents. The lift back into the river is down a steep bank on the left, below the factory.

The river is re-entered 1 mile above the I-91 bridge. The remaining portion of this trip is in tobacco-farming country that becomes more urban as Hartford is approached. In 3 miles, the Scantic River enters on the left and, 2 miles farther, is Windsor, with its interesting old houses. Here the Farmington River enters on the right. In another 4 miles, the Podunk River enters on the left. One has a fine view of the Hartford skyline on the right for the next 3 miles to the Charter Oak Bridge, where the Hockanum River enters on the left and brings in a certain amount of pollution. In another 2½ miles, the Wethersfield Cove opens up on the right under the I-91 bridge. There is a public landing on the south side of the Cove, and some of the fine old houses of the town, which are open to the public, are well worth a visit.

Wethersfield Cove—Middletown   **15 mi**

Description:	**Flatwater,** quickwater, tidal
Date checked:	1985
Navigable:	Passable at all water levels
Scenery:	Rural, forested, settled, urban
Maps:	USGS Hartford South, Glastonbury, Middle Haddam, Middletown

Although the lower part of this river is tidal, the tides have little effect until Middletown, and are not really important until Hadlyme. In the 7 miles to the Rocky Hill Ferry, the river meanders across a broad flood plain. The banks are generally low and sandy with fields and woods offering good picnic or camping places. Just above Rocky Hill, below an abutment of large rocks, is the Hall's Landing marina. For the next 8 miles to Middletown the river's course is straighter and the countryside is hillier. Gildersleeve Island, 5 miles below the Ferry, offers suitable camping spots, while Riverside Marine Park, on the right bank, has picnic tables and a launching area. In another 2½ miles, just above the mouth of the Mattabessett River in Middletown, Wilcox Island offers campsites. At the CT 6A bridge there is a landing place on the right.

Middletown—Old Saybrook   27^1/$_2$ mi

Description:	**Tidal**
Date checked:	1989, WB, SG
Scenery:	Forested, settled
Maps:	USGS Middletown, Middle Haddam, Haddam, Deep River, Essex, Old Lyme
Campsites:	6^3/$_4$ mi L Hurd State Park
	11 mi L Gillette Castle State Park
	17^1/$_2$+ mi L Selden Neck State Park

A few of the access points are listed here:

West bank—	0 mi	Middletown launching area off CT 9
West bank—	11 mi	Haddam Meadows State Park (south end) off CT 9A
East bank—	ca.11 mi	Haddam Neck nuclear plant
East bank—	13 mi	Salmon River launching area off CT 149
East bank—	13^3/$_4$ mi	Goodspeed Opera parking lot off CT 149
West bank—	16^1/$_2$ mi	Chester ferry landing
West bank—	22^1/$_4$ mi	Essex town dock
West bank—	27^1/$_2$ mi	mouth of South Cove in Old Saybrook from CT 154

For information and specific regulations concerning these access areas and campsites write *well in advance* to State of Connecticut, Department of Environmental Protection, Office of Parks and Recreation, Hartford, CT 06115. Ask for the "Canoe Camping" leaflet.

Below Middletown the river changes. It deepens and widens as it winds through the hilly country of southern Connecticut. The banks, high and ledgy, are more heavily forested. South of Middletown all property within the sight lines of the river is in the Connecticut River Gateway, an attempt by the state to maintain the scenic value of the river.

This lower part of the Connecticut River can be paddled any time of the year that it is ice free, but the best times are before Memorial Day and after Labor Day, when powerboats with heavy wakes are less in evidence.

Rather than follow the main river all the way, a more interesting route is to paddle the "back alleys" that parallel the river. They lie along the east side of the river in East Haddam, Lyme, and Old Lyme. In addition, there are several attractive coves in the same area. The most helpful maps for paddling behind the islands and in the coves are the USGS Deep River and Old Lyme sheets.

The back alleys along the east shore begin below the CT 82 bridge (13³/4 mi). Keep to the left of Rich Island (14¹/2 mi) and enter Chapman Pond from the west and leave it at the south end. The next one begins below the ferry crossing and extends to the east of Selden Neck (17¹/4 mi) via Selden Cove and Selden Creek. It is in Selden Cove that the citizens of Essex hid their ships from the British raiding parties during the War of 1812. There are more such passages above the Connecticut Turnpike (I-95) (25 mi) and below the railroad bridge.

The river can be idyllic at times, but summer weekends can be a madhouse with heavy powerboat congestion. Many boaters do not observe accepted etiquette and canoes are not given right-of-way. Boat wakes in narrow stretches can mimic whitewater and novices should beware. It is recommended that non-swimmers **wear** PFDs. The wind and tide can also be powerful adversaries. The tide stage at Old Saybrook can be learned from most newspapers. The tides at Essex, East Haddam, and Middletown follow Old Saybrook by approximately 1, 2, and 5 hours, respectively.

MILLERS RIVER   MA

The Millers River flows west into the Connecticut River near Greenfield. It has several sections that provide distinctly different types of canoeing. Above Royalston there are many miles of smoothwater paddling; from South Royalston to Athol there are continuous, intermediate rapids; the stretch from Athol to Erving is mostly slackwater; and from Erving to Millers Falls the river has a mixture of easy and heavy rapids. The water of the Millers is naturally dark.

Several miles of the river above Winchendon are probably canoeable in high water, but they are mostly through swamp. Through Winchendon, there is a series of millponds, dams, and rapids. The last dam is at Waterville on MA 202.

Waterville—South Royalston   **11 mi**

Description:	Flatwater, **quickwater,** Class I
Date checked:	1985
Navigable:	High water
Scenery:	Forested, towns
Maps:	USGS Winchendon, Royalston
Portages:	9¹/₂ mi dam Flood control dam
	(11 mi dam)

One can put in just below the Waterville dam on a side road, but the first mile is obstructed by shallow rapids, a broken (but runnable) dam, and brush jams. Below the rapids, a branch enters from the north. It is small but canoeable in high water from State Line on MA 12, with some portages around dams and obstructions. Below this junction, the Winchendon sewage disposal plant is passed on the left.

The recommended starting point is the bridge at Hydeville. The next bridge is on New Boston Road, 5 miles along. The river winds through swamp and woodlands, with almost no current, but is fairly pleasant if the water is not too low. All of this section is in the reservoir of the Birch Hill flood-control dam, in which the Massachusetts Department of Conservation is pursuing an extensive fish and wildlife management and improvement program. One mile below New Boston Road, the Otter River enters from the south, and 2 miles farther, the Birch Hill Dam is reached. It is another 1¹/₂ miles to the dam at South Royalston.

South Royalston-Athol   **6³/₄ mi**

Description:	Class III
Date checked:	1985
Navigable:	High water: late March, early April
	Medium water: late April
Scenery:	Forested
Maps:	USGS Royalston, Athol

This popular whitewater run, known as the Upper Millers, consists of a number of Class III rapids. The amount of water in this section is controlled by the Birch Hill Flood Control Dam, and a check on the volume can be made by calling the Army Corps of Engineers (508-249-4467) at the dam. A scratchy run can be made with as little as 500 cfs, but more water is really desirable. At 1200 cfs, an open boat, singly paddled, is still suitable; it is estimated that 1600 cfs would require a heavy-water boat.

A put-in can be made at the green MA 68 bridge, but there is a broken dam that can be rocky and dangerous at the wrong water level just above the next bridge in Royalston. Look it over carefully.

The better put-in is from a side road 1/2 mile below the MA 68 bridge on the right. Rapids begin immediately and pass around islands, then the pace slackens briefly before plunging into a wavy Class III drop at the first railroad bridge (1 mi). Another short, flat stretch leads into a sharp left turn and a mile of continuous Class III rapids.

There is a right turn and some smoothwater under the second railroad bridge (3 mi). Just below is the site of the old Bear's Den Bridge. The easy rapids that follow include a little drop next to the railroad. In the next mile, the rapids increase through Hemlock Gorge, a Class III section. The rapids then moderate, gradually flattening out in the pool above the dam in Athol (6³/4 mi).

A rough take-out is necessary on the right bank—through the brush and along an old wood road to a side road. In Athol you must portage three dams to continue downstream.

Athol—Erving   11 mi

Maps:	USGS Athol, Orange, Millers Falls

Below the dams in Athol, the river is flat to the dam at Orange. Below Orange, the river leaves the flat valley and flows between steep hills again. The next dam is at Wendell Depot. There are only a few rapids in this section. The dam at Erving Paper Mills is broken, but it cannot be run. Then there is smoothwater to a low dam at Erving, which can be run.

Erving—Millers Falls   6 mi

Description:	Class **II**-IV
Date checked:	1989, KD, LD
Navigable:	High water: March, April
	Medium water: May
Scenery:	Forested, settled
Maps:	USGS Millers Falls
Portage:	3^1/$_4$ mi E Funnel 150 yd (optional)

This popular whitewater run is referred to as the Lower Millers. It can be run late in the spring when other nearby rivers are too low and often even later in the season after heavy rains. The gradient is not as steep as the Upper Millers, but the waves are larger.

The start can be made at an old bridge on a side road in Erving or one mile below at a pull-off next to a railroad bridge. Heavy water Class II rapids lead from the railroad bridge to the old bridge at Farley (2^1/$_2$ mi), where the gauge is found on the right. A Class III rapid, best run on the left, is found just below the bridge. Class II rapids lead to another Class III rapid with large rocks on the left, followed by a pool. Take out toward the end of the pool on the right to scout the Funnel. The Funnel is a Class IV rapid at most water levels, and it should be walked by all but expert boaters. Two large boulders form holes in midstream, with large waves and abrupt drops throughout. The rapid is runnable on the extreme left, the extreme right, and down the middle, but pick your line carefully. The river then approaches the road on a high bank and passes through another Class III rapid. It is suggested that boaters take out here and carry up to a rest area.

Moderate rapids continue to the broken dam at the Millers Falls Paper Company (5^1/$_4$ mi), which should be scouted and run with caution, if at all. There is debris in this area, more so on the left side. The current pushes you left. Rapids continue through Millers Falls, with a strong rapid below the MA 63 bridge at a broken dam. Take out at an old millyard on the right (6 mi). It is possible to paddle diminishing rapids another 1^3/$_4$ miles to the Connecticut River, where a bridge on a side road provides a possible take-out.

OTTER RIVER MA

Maps:	USGS Templeton, Winchendon

The Otter River is a short stream rising in Templeton and flowing north into the Millers River above South Royalston. A water treatment plant under construction in Templeton is expected to improve the quality of the water substantially in both rivers.

From the MA 2A bridge it is 3³/₄ miles of moderate current past the MA 101 bridge and through mostly wooded countryside to the broken dam just above the River Street bridge in Otter River Village. Lift over the center of the 8-foot dam.

There is another dam above the Depot Street bridge (4³/₄ mi) in Otter River Village. Portage on the right or paddle along the canal on the left and carry out to the street.

There are a few rapids to the US 202 bridge in Baldwinville (6¹/₂ mi). The remains of an old dam just below this bridge form a couple of small Class II-III drops.

In the last 3¹/₄ miles to the Millers River (9³/₄ mi), there is a fair current with no hazards. The river is mostly in meadows and within the ponding area of the Birch Hill Flood Control Dam (11¹/₄ mi) on the Millers River.

TULLY RIVER MA

Maps:	USGS Royalston, Athol

The Tully River is a tributary of the Millers River just west of Athol. It is mostly smoothwater with some Class I and II rapids. Start a trip by going about 2¹/₂ miles north of Athol on MA 32, and turning west onto Fryeville Road. Begin at the bridge over the East Branch.

The first ¹/₄ mile below Fryeville Road is narrow, shallow, and rapid, passable only at high water. The next mile to a broken dam is flat. The broken dam can be run, or it can be portaged on the right. Then there is fast current for 200 yards to the Pinedale Avenue bridge (1¹/₄ mi). The West Branch joins below, and there is mostly flatwater to the Millers River ($3^1/2$ mi). There is a bridge less than $^1/4$ mile downstream. *Scouted only.*

FALLS RIVER   MA

Maps:	USGS Bernardston, Greenfield

The Falls River is a small stream that rises in Guilford, Vermont, and flows south through Bernardston to the Connecticut River at Turners Falls. Above Bernardston village, it is too small for canoeing. There are long deadwaters caused by dams in Bernardston and 1 mile below at Hoe Shop Road. The best part of the river is below this second dam, but even here the trip requires high water. No roads follow the river and the banks are steep and wooded. Much of the land on both sides is posted against trespassing.

Bernardston—Factory Village   4 mi

From the MA 10 bridge it is largely deadwater to the dam 1 mile below. The next mile to Bascom Road is mostly rapid, but not difficult. Carry left around an impassable ledge, $^1/4$ mile below the Bascom Road bridge. There are some good rapids a mile below here, near the Boy Scout camp on the right. Then the hills close in and form a small canyon. In less than a mile of easy paddling, one comes to a picnic ground and a dam, which is portaged on the right. Below the dam is $^1/2$ mile of fast current and easy rapids to the clearing above Gill Road. **Caution!** Proceed with care here, as the rapids increase to an impassable falls just above the bridge. Take out on the right. The last $^1/4$ mile to the Connecticut River is probably not canoeable.

DEERFIELD RIVER   MA

The Deerfield River rises east of the Green Mountains in southern Vermont and flows south into Massachusetts, where it turns east to join the Connecticut River near Greenfield. Although it has been developed for power, good sections of rapids remain. The section from Monroe Bridge to Bear Swamp Reservoir, presently only rarely runnable due to diversions, may have scheduled releases in the future. Large dams are found in the headwaters at Somerset and Whitingham in Vermont. There is a large dam a mile above Monroe Bridge, a small one at Monroe Bridge, and a large one at the Bear Swamp facility below Monroe Bridge. The power company has not been cooperative in providing information about releases.

Monroe Bridge—Bear Swamp Reservoir 4 mi

Description:	Class IV
Date checked:	1989, JC
Navigable:	High water: early spring, when other rivers are in flood
	Dam controlled: Historically difficult to get information
Scenery:	Wild
Map:	USGS Rowe

Put in on the left below the dam in Monroe Bridge. Because the put-in is down an extremely steep bank, throw ropes are suggested. The Deerfield hits its first Class III drop immediately below. Fine play spots continue for a mile to the harder section, where several Class IV drops appear in pool-drop succession to the reservoir. The best drop might be called Dragon's Teeth, after the rocks spaced along river left. It plunges straight ahead through a mega-hole and ends in either a fine pop-up spot or large standing waves, depending upon the water level. Because the reservoir rises and falls as much as fifteen feet during the day, you may find the last drop drowned. Take out on the right and scramble carefully over the rocks to the road. The take-out is as rough as any in New England. You are on private power-company property, so be courteous. Carry your boat through the forest to the left of the first fence you find, then up the road to the parking lot at the picnic area. Park your car in the picnic area, as they close the gates without warning.

Bear Swamp Dam—MA 2 Bridge   8¹/₂ mi

Description:	Quickwater, Class I, II
Date checked:	1985
Navigable:	Medium water when New England Power is generating power
Scenery:	Forested, rural
Map:	USGS Rowe
Portage:	4³/₄ mi R Zoar Gap (optional)

This part of the river is beautiful. The river valley is quite steep in many places, with the Berkshire Hills rising from the river. There is a road, however, all along the river.

The put-in is 1¹/₄ miles above the Hoosac Tunnel and just below the Bear Swamp Dam. As the road turns to the left, go straight onto the old road river. This area is reached from MA 2—the Mohawk Trail—by taking the River Road to Zoar at the east end of the MA 2 bridge, where it crosses over the Deerfield, west of the town of Charlemont.

About 5 miles of quickwater, Class I and II, lead to Zoar Gap from the put-in. Zoar Gap is *exceedingly difficult* to recognize from above and has been the site of many serious accidents. It cannot be recognized by the sound of the rapids (nor can many other trouble spots, although people still keep trying!). Nor is it feasible to rely on signs. If you can't spend the time to scout this spot on your way *upstream*, then start your trip at the River Road bridge.

Zoar Gap is a Class III-IV rapid extending about 50 feet. Scout it from shore. It can be lined on the right shore. The easiest route to run is close to the right shore until you are even with the heavy hydraulics that are in the center; then shoot out to the center just below the hydraulics to avoid a rock hidden by heavy water close to shore on the right. Although you can run the gap in the center, you are likely to submerge an open canoe.

Right below Zoar Gap are the River Road Bridge and the Electric Company Roadside Park on the left. This makes a good lunch spot or put-in for a shorter trip, if you want to avoid Zoar Gap. From here to the MA 2 take-out is easy Class II with some large rocks and some ripples; the river is wide. The take-out is just below the MA 2 bridge on the left at the roadside rest area.

MA 2 Bridge—First Dam at Shelburne Falls $8^1/_2$ mi

Description:	Flatwater, quickwater, Class I
Date checked:	1985
Navigable:	Low water when New England Power is generating power
Scenery:	Rural, towns
Maps:	USGS Rowe, Heath, Ashfield, Shelburne Falls, Colrain

The river is wide and shallow in this area. At a couple of points only one channel has enough water for a canoe, so the most difficult part of the trip is reading the river and finding the water. It is a good, easy river for beginning whitewater.

Put in west of the town of Charlemont at the Roadside Rest Area just before MA 2 crosses the river. From there the river provides an easy run with fine riffles. As you approach the center of Charlemont, you pass under the MA 8A bridge; MA 2—the Mohawk Trail—is close to the river all the way. As you near the take-out, the river becomes deadwater held back by the dam at Shelburne Falls. The take-out is a public boat ramp on the left about a mile above the dam.

Through Shelburne 7 mi

There are four dams above and below Shelburne Falls, with Class II-III rapids below the third dam.

Bardwell Bridge—Connecticut River 12 mi

Description:	Quickwater, Class I
Date checked:	1985
Navigable:	Dam controlled, medium water
Scenery:	Settled
Maps:	USGS Shelburne Falls, Colrain

This section can be run in the summer as a swimming trip. It is mostly quickwater, with only one fun Class I rapid.

There are 4 miles of river with a few rapids and riffles to the mouth of the South River on the right. The river continues unobstructed for another 3 miles in its narrow valley, with an average drop of 20 feet per mile. Near Wapping, it suddenly breaks out into open farmland and becomes mostly flat. The next 4 miles to the mouth of the Green River (on the left near Greenfield) and then another 2 miles to the Connecticut River make a good, easy paddle.

DEERFIELD RIVER, North Branch   VT

Known locally as the Dover Branch, this stream rises in Dover, Vermont, and flows southwesterly through Wilmington to the northeast corner of Harriman Reservoir. It flows through scenic farm country with fine views of Haystack Mountain, and the water itself is sparkling clear.

This branch provides a fine early spring run of moderate difficulty, mainly fastwater with some Class II rapids and two Class III pitches of short duration. It is easier than the Northwest Branch.

Off VT 100—Harriman Reservoir   6 mi

Description:	Quickwater, Class I, II, III
Date checked:	1985
Navigable:	High water: late April through mid-May
Scenery:	Rural, town
Map:	USGS Wilmington 15

Put in 4½ miles northeast of the center of Wilmington Village off VT 100, where a farm road leads down to the river across the end of a meadow below a bridge. The stream is narrow but clear with a fast current. There are frequent riffles and mild Class II rapids. After passing under the cement bridge on VT 100 (3 mi), the stream swings to the right around a large meadow and, after bearing left at the edge of a sugar orchard, descends over Class II rapids of moderate difficulty. These are about ¼ mile long and are best run on the left.

The river then levels off until entering the narrow, steep Class III chute that channels it through the center of the village. There is a sharp turn to the left at the head of this rapid, then a straight run down to the bridge in the center of town. This should be scouted before running.

Below the remains of an old mill dam, the stream becomes wider and swifter as it parallels VT 9. There are some Class II rapids that require caution in very high water. A short distance above Harriman Reservoir (the distance varies depending on the height of water impounded), there is another Class III pitch that should be scouted carefully. Unless there is sufficient water to cover the boulder-filled runout below this rapid, take out opposite the electric power relay station on VT 9 (6 mi).

DEERFIELD RIVER, Northwest Branch   VT

Map:	USGS Wilmington 15

This stream rises to the west of Somerset Reservoir and runs southerly to join the outlet of the reservoir a short distance above the lower dam where the penstock takes off to the Searsburg generating station. Take the road from VT 9 west of Wilmington toward the Somerset Dam, following the wooden penstock to the lower dam. Note carefully the conditions at the pond above this dam. Canoes must be taken out well above the lip of the dam, where the stream drops a sheer 120 feet. About 4 miles above, the road crosses the Northwest Branch, and this is a good launching spot.

The run from the put-in to the pond above the lower dam is about 5 miles of uninterrupted Class II and Class III rapids, making a fine whitewater run at the height of the spring runoff. The country here is wild and beautiful, the water clear over a rocky bottom, and herds of deer are often seen at this time of year.

DEERFIELD RIVER, West Branch   VT

This is one of the most difficult whitewater runs for the expert boater in the northeast. Gradient alone tells the story. The upper section drops 114 feet per mile, and the lower section drops 192 feet per mile. Not included in these calculations is the Class VI middle section, which drops 60 feet in 1000 feet, better than 300 feet per mile. If you love horizon lines, technical rapids, horrible places to swim, and the biggest take-out high you've ever had, this is your river.

Readsboro Falls—Deerfield River   **3 mi**

Description:	Class IV, V, VI
Date checked:	1989, JC
Navigable:	High water: March - early May
Scenery:	Forested, settled
Map:	USGS Wilmington
Portage:	$1^3/4$ mi R Class VI section 500 yd

The put-in is reached by travelling west on VT 8 about 3 miles to a gravel road on the left between a barn and a house. This is Readsboro Falls. Put in below the falls to avoid the strange hydraulic that causes boats to pencil up and down but not out. Just down from the put-in is a 350-yard rapid. Stop under the bridge to scout the 5-foot drop and 50 yards of rapids that follow. Although the next drop looks unrunnable, it can be run on the left. The river then drops to a pool and over a three-foot drop, then comes up against a large boulder that splits the current. It is suggested that this drop be avoided on river left. From here to the pullover above the Class VI section on the right is an easy run. The Class VI section, called Tunnel Vision, has been run, but it is not recommended.

The lower section starts just after the river emerges from the tunnel under the road. After the first drop is a large waterfall on the right. The river splits here, with safe passage only on the left. From this point to a park on the right about $1/4$ mile away, the river drops extremely fast and is very technical. Scout this section if you have any doubts about your abilities.

As you paddle into town, two rapids should get all of your attention. The first, High Chair, is at the upper corner of the old wooden chair factory. This should be scouted. The big rock near the building where the river turns sharply right is undercut, and poses problems in low water. Low Chair follows below the bridge, and it should also be scouted. If you have any doubts about this one, do not attempt it. If you do decide to run it, start on the right, drop about three feet, and then cross to the left to hit the chute between the shore and the first big boulder. It can also be run on the right. The take-out is just below on the left above the Deerfield River.

The gauge is found at the bridge by the chair factory, looking upstream, on the left. It is barely runnable at zero, and best at five.

COLD RIVER   MA

The Cold River flows into the Deerfield near Charlemont. The Mohawk Trail (MA 2) follows the lower section, but most of the rapids are not visible from the highway. The river is known for its steep gradient and technical drops. It is runnable in the early spring or after heavy rains.

South County Road—MA 2   6 mi

Description:	Class II, III
Date checked:	1989, JC
Navigable:	High water: mid-March, April
Scenery:	Wild
Maps:	USGS North Adams, Rowe

This is a beautiful section to paddle, with a very easy put-in. The take-out above the Class IV water, however, is unspeakable. Be prepared to portage around the occasional strainer. Although the gradient is 100 feet per mile, it is almost evenly distributed, so there are no big drops. At the take-out, be alert for the MA 2 guardrail high on the left. This is the end of the Class II-III section, and the beginning of the Class IV section.

To find the put-in, drive west on MA 2 up the mountain to a small settlement. This is Drury. Turn south and continue straight until the road crosses a small stream. This is the Cold River.

MA 2 Hairpin Turn—Deerfield River   4¹/₂ mi

Description:	Class IV
Date checked:	1989, JC
Navigable:	High water: mid-March, April
Scenery:	Wild
Maps:	USGS North Adams, Rowe
Portage:	4¹/₄ mi R waterfall 20 yd
	(runnable at higher levels)

This section has been called one of the best whitewater runs in the East. The upper and lower sections have a gradient of 130 feet per mile, and the middle section has a gradient of 100 feet per mile. It is technical in nature and demands good boat control.

A gauge is located on the green bridge at the Mohawk Trail State Forest campground, on the downstream side of the left pillar. Low water is minus one to plus two. Medium levels are three to six, and high is above seven. When the gauge is in double digits, the Cold is Class V.

To reach the upper section of this run, travel west from the campground to a bridge. Drive up the mountain 1 mile to the hairpin curve, turn around where you can, then return to the hairpin. Unload the boats as fast as you can and leave. It is dangerous to linger in the road here. Use throw lines to lower your boats down to the river. The first big drop, High Anxiety, is where the river disappears in a left hand turn. Scout on the right. Fifty yards below is a river-wide hole, which must be run on the extreme left at high water; otherwise, it becomes a keeper. The Savoy Shuffle leads to the bridge, the start of the middle section.

The first rapid in the middle section, Cuisinart, starts just after the bridge, and it is one of the longest and toughest on the river. An alternate put-in is just below this rapid, at a large parking lot. Several rapids below Cuisinart is Pinball, where several large boulders channel the water into a narrow sluiceway on the left. Stay left of the red rock. While it looks formidable, this is the easiest route.

The lower section starts at the green bridge. There is a large waterfall 1/4 mile below the bridge. Portage on the right or run it on the right at high water. Watch out for Joe's Rock at the bottom of the drop.

A small stream entering on the right creates an eddy on the right. The best route for the next rapid is on the left. The last rapid is Landing Zone. Start on the left, cross over to the extreme right, and drop into the hole. Although this move looks impossible, it can be done.

NORTH RIVER   VT, MA

The North River rises in southern Vermont and flows south into the Deerfield River. The section above Halifax Gorge is too small for canoeing. MA 112 follows the river, providing many access points.

Halifax Gorge—Colrain   7 mi

Description:	Class I, **II**, III
Date checked:	1986, ST
Navigable:	High water: early spring, after heavy rains
Scenery:	Forested, rural
Map:	USGS Colrain

It is possible to put in from VT 112 a mile north of the Massachusetts-Vermont state line where the road leaves the river and goes up a steep hill. The first three drops are Class III, and novices might elect to put in below. The next 2 miles to the upper MA 112 bridge contains continuous Class II rapids. The 5 miles from the upper MA 112 bridge to the MA 112 bridge at Colrain is wider and, for the most part, gentler, with an occasional harder rapid.

Colrain—Deerfield River   6 mi

Below Colrain, the river flows through a more heavily populated and industrialized region and has less attractive scenery and more polluted water. There are two portages and two Class III rapids as well as several Class II sections.

Put in at a field just upstream of the MA 112 bridge at Colrain across MA 112 from the Colrain School. A mile below at a sharp left turn is a broken dam and tight rapid, which may be run with caution (Class III at medium water). There is an iron bridge just below the broken dam.

For the next mile the rapids diminish, the river goes under a covered bridge, and then soon enters the slackwater of a large dam above Griswoldville. The West Branch enters on the right; it is small and steep, and is probably not canoeable. Portage left 1/4 mile along MA 112 around the dam and mill. The river becomes polluted below here, and 2 miles of minor rapids lead to Shattuckville. Here the river narrows and there is a small waterfall that must be portaged left. A short way below, just above the high bridge at Shattuckville, is a bad pitch, which should be looked over or lined down on the right. Continuous rapids of intermediate difficulty continue 1 mile to the Deerfield River. One can take out at the bridge here, or continue down the Deerfield.

GREEN RIVER   VT, MA

The Green River is a crystal mountain stream that descends a narrow valley through the hills north of Greenfield, Massachusetts, and empties into the Deerfield River near that city. Rising to the west of Governors Mountain in Guilford, Vermont, it is large enough to canoe in freshet by the time it reaches Green River Post Office. There are excellent swimming holes and plenty of opportunities for trout fishing. It is an unusually beautiful stream and a delight to the nature lover.

Green River—West Leyden   6¼ mi

Description:	Class III
Date checked:	1985
Navigable:	High water: early April
Scenery:	Forested
Maps:	USGS Brattleboro, Colrain
Portage:	5¼ mi L dam

The access and car shuttle are as difficult as the canoeing on the Green River, because the best water level for canoeing coincides with the last part of mud season. Although a dirt road follows immediately along the right bank, it is often impassable for all except four-wheel-drive vehicles. The worst part is in the vicinity of the state line. The long way around continues north from the covered bridge past the turn to West Leyden. Avoid the dirt short cut and take the turn ½ mile south of Guilford Center. Only the last mile down to the river is still unimproved.

A canoe can be launched a short distance above Green River. The usual start is on the dirt road on the right bank. All of the pitches can be run at ordinary high water levels, but the river is small, steep, and full of ledges, particularly in the upper part where it rounds Pulpet Mountain. It is best to proceed cautiously, checking each chute before you run it.

The Massachusetts state line is passed at 3¼ miles. At Stewartsville the dam at the sawmill is best carried on the left.

West Leyden—Water-Supply Dam   5¾ mi

Description:	Class I, II
Date checked:	1985
Navigable:	High water: early April
Scenery:	Forested
Maps:	USGS Colrain, Bernardston
Portage:	(7 mi L dam)

From West Leyden to the next bridge is a delightful run. Here the rapids are almost continuous but never severe. There are many clear, deep pools, beautiful banks, and steep, wooded hillsides. Canoes may be launched from the right bank just below the bridge at West Leyden. The most difficult drop is about halfway down and can cause trouble, especially at high water. Pull out 7 miles below on the left, just above the Greenfield water-supply dam.

Water-Supply Dam—Greenfield   6 mi

Description:	Flatwater, quickwater, Class I
Date checked:	1985
Navigable:	Medium water
Scenery:	Forested, rural
Maps:	USGS Bernardston, Greenfield

A covered bridge crosses the river at the start. Rapids are few, but the current snakes busily around undercutting trees, creating a real hazard for the canoeist. Here the river leaves its narrow valley and passes through flat, farming country to its junction with the Deerfield River.

CHICOPEE RIVER   MA

The Chicopee River springs from the merger of the Quaboag and Ware rivers at Three Rivers in Palmer. It flows west to the Connecticut River at Chicopee. It drops 220 feet in $16^{3}/_{4}$ miles, but ten dams in that distance make nearly all of it smooth-water paddling. These dams limit the appeal of this river.

Three River—Ludlow 8¹/₄ **mi**

Description:	**Flatwater,** Class I-III
Date checked:	1985
Navigable:	Passable at most water levels
Scenery:	Forested, urban
Maps:	USGS Palmer, Ludlow, Springfield North
Portages:	2³/₄ mi L Red Bridge Dam 100 yd
	5 mi R dam at North Wilbraham 50 yd

Flood prevention work in Three Rivers has led to the removal of the old dams there. Considerable blasting has filled the first ¹/₂ mile of the Chicopee with very sharp rocks and large haystacks. This section of Class III rapids should be looked over before running. Below this drop is a 2-mile-long polluted impoundment that ends at Red Bridge Dam. In contrast to the water quality, beautiful hemlock, white pine, and mountain laurel line the shores.

At Red Bridge (2³/₄ mi), take out on the left bank just above the dam, portage along Red Bridge Road, and put in from the right bank just below the powerhouse. There is a short Class II rapid and then more flatwater until you reach the dam at North Wilbraham (5 mi). Carry on the right bank. Below the dam is another brief Class II rapid, followed by flatwater to the third dam (8¹/₄ mi) in Ludlow. Take out on the left bank on River Road near the point where the boundaries of Ludlow, Springfield, and Wilbraham meet.

Ludlow—Chicopee 8¹/₂ **mi**

There are about a half-dozen dams in the remaining 8¹/₂ miles to the Connecticut River in Chicopee, so the last half of the river is not recommended.

WARE RIVER   MA

The Ware River rises near Hubbardston and flows in a southwesterly direction to Three Rivers, where, within a mile, it joins with the Quaboag and Swift rivers to form the Chicopee River.

Much of it flows through a relatively unspoiled part of the state, but the upper section is very overgrown. Improvements have been made in the water quality, making summer canoeing, which is generally possible below MA 32 in Barre Plains, more pleasant than it once was.

Barre Falls—South Barre   6 mi

Description:	Flatwater, quickwater, Class I, II
Date checked:	1985
Navigable:	Ponds canoeable most water levels
Scenery:	Forested, settled
Map:	USGS Barre
Portages:	3³/₄ mi R Quabbin diversion ³/₄ mi
	(6 mi R dam)

This section of river might best be considered as two flatwater sections. The carry down from the road at Barre Falls Dam is difficult, and the small stream is canoeable only at high water. The river can next be reached at the covered bridge site (1³/₄ mi). Since the road is rough dirt and the next 2 miles of river are almost flat through a wild area of bays, it might best be enjoyed by paddling upstream from the access at the MA 122 bridge near Coldbrook Springs (3³/₄ mi).

Since boating is not allowed above the Coldbrook Diversion Dam, portage by car to below the second dam, if canoeing on the river, or to Powder Mill Pond, which lies between White Valley and the dam at South Barre.

South Barre—Wheelwright   4¹/₄ mi

Description:	Flatwater, Class I-II
Date checked:	1985
Navigable:	Passable at most water levels
Scenery:	Forested, towns
Maps:	USGS Barre, North Brookfield, Ware
Portages:	4¹/₄ mi L dam at Wheelwright 20 yd

There is a short rapid below the South Barre dam, and then the river divides, forcing canoeists to choose the less-obstructed channel. The last 3 miles from Barre Plains and the MA 32 bridge (1¼ mi) are pleasant as the river slows gradually to the paper-mill dam at Wheelwright (4½ mi).

Wheelwright—Ware 10½ mi

Description:	Flatwater, **quickwater,** Class II, III
Date checked:	1985
Navigable:	High or medium water: spring
	Low water: passable for flatwater sections
Scenery:	Forested
Map:	USGS Ware
Portages:	(10½ mi L three dams in Ware ½ mi)

This section of the Ware River is a pleasant flatwater trip broken in half by nearly 2 miles of rapids. It is possible for both flatwater and whitewater paddlers to arrange shorter trips to their liking.

In Gilbertville there is a gauge on the downstream side of the right abutment of the Upper Church Street bridge. At a reading of 11.5 and above, the rapids at Gilbertville are barely navigable. Note that on this particular gauge, higher numbers correspond to lower water levels.

From the Wheelwright dam, 2 miles of flatwater and occasional riffles lead to the bridge on the Barre Airport road. After a little drop underneath this bridge, there is smoothwater for ½ mile to a railroad bridge (2½ mi). Through wooded banks and mountain laurel, the river flows gently for 1¼ miles to a side-road bridge (3¾ mi). Since there is no easy take-out right above the rapids, boaters desiring only flatwater should take out here.

In another 2 miles you reach the third railroad bridge (5¾ mi), just below which Class II-III rapids begin. These rapids can be impassable in low water. On the whole, the rapids above the MA 32 bridge (6½ mi) in Gilbertville are somewhat harder than the mile after this bridge. From the covered bridge in Gilbertville (6¾ mi) the rapids diminish, giving way to quickwater for the remaining distance to the Upper Church Street bridge (8½ mi).

The last 2 miles to Ware are flat and somewhat wider. Grenville Park, $^1/_2$ mile above the first dam ($10^1/_2$ mi) in Ware, provides a number of take-outs with easy automobile access.

If you are continuing downstream, portage the three dams in Ware together. Under no condition should you put in below the first dam, since heavy rapids and concrete retaining walls make the stretch hazardous. For a carry on foot, pull out on the left just above the first dam, cross the bridge below the dam, continue through the center of town, turn left on West Street, and take the first alley on the left leading to the river (11 mi).

Ware—Three Rivers $11^1/_4$ mi

Description:	Flatwater, **quickwater,** Class I, II, III
Date checked:	1985
Navigable:	Passable whenever ice-free, except below dams
Scenery:	Forested, urban
Maps:	USGS Ware, Palmer
Portages:	$8^1/_4$ mi L 1st dam at Thorndike 20 yd
	$8^3/_4$ mi L 2nd dam in Thorndike

From Ware to Thorndike there are $8^1/_4$ miles of fine quickwater canoeing with a strong current and several good riffles. The MA 32 bridge is passed $3^1/_4$ miles below Ware. At Thorndike ($8^1/_4$ mi) there are two dams, both of which should be portaged on the left. After the first dam and a road bridge, there is a short Class III rapid, which can be tricky in low water or heavy in high water.

The last 3 miles to Three Rivers contain a couple of Class II-III rapids, particularly right after the second dam in Thorndike. Below MA 181 (10 mi) the Swift River enters on the right ($10^1/_2$ mi). Then it is $^3/_4$ mile to Three Rivers, where the Quaboag and Ware rivers meet to form the Chicopee River ($11^1/_4$ mi).

WARE RIVER, West Branch   MA

The Ware River is formed at the junction of the East and West branches just above the Barre Falls Flood Control Dam. A large network of dirt roads winds through the area, but the dam is most easily reached from MA 62 by a paved road to the picnic area and canoe launch south of the dam. While a canoe can be worked down from above Hubbardston, most people paddle upstream from the dam on either the East or West Branch. The water level and the energy of the paddler determine the distance that it is possible to paddle upstream.

WARE RIVER, East Branch   MA

This is a small stream, barely a canoe-length wide, and often obstructed by trees and bushes. While it has been run from the ponds above MA 62, even the section described below is not recommended except for adventure.

North Rutland—Barre Falls   5¹/₂ mi

Description:	Flatwater, **quickwater,** Class II
Date checked:	1985
Navigable:	Medium and high water: late March through May
Scenery:	Forested, town
Maps:	USGS Wachusett Mountain, Barre
Portages:	2¹/₂ mi dam site at New Boston
	(5¹/₂ mi L flood control dam

Put in below the last dam in North Rutland. The first 2¹/₂ miles to New Boston provide interesting and varied running, but expect some brush. First is a good Class II rapid, which is easier in higher water. The current continues strong with some easy, intermittent Class II rapids followed by more strong current through swampy country. An easily run 1-foot dam and about a mile of smoothwater bring you to New Boston (2¹/₂ mi). The milldam is gone, and the drop exposed may have to be carried at most reasonable water levels. The river gradually becomes less steep and slows in the next 3 miles to Barre Falls Flood Control Dam (5¹/₂ mi). **Caution!** Do not cross the log boom or in any way enter the intake channel for the 885-foot-long dam. There is no permanent lake behind this dam, and the stream is allowed to flow directly through a chute and tunnel in the dam. Five canoeists were injured here in 1975 when they were accidentally washed through or became hung up on the dam. Take out on the left.

SWIFT RIVER   MA

The runnable upper stretches of the Swift River and its branches have all been inundated by the Quabbin Reservoir, which supplies Greater Boston. Regulations of the Metropolitan District Commission prohibit the use of canoes, sailboats, collapsible boats, and inboards on the Quabbin Reservoir. Therefore, boating is limited to the section of the Swift River below Winsor Dam.

The portion of the run immediately below the Quabbin Reservoir is the most attractive. The banks are heavily forested and the water is clear. Unfortunately, the river is quickly polluted and there are several dams in Bondsville.

MA 9—Three Rivers $8^3/_4$ mi

Description:	Flatwater, Class I
Date checked:	1985
Navigable:	Passable at anytime after ice-out
	Dam-controlled
Scenery:	Forested, towns
Maps:	USGS Winsor Dam, Palmer
Portages:	1 mi R broken dam at West Ware
	$4^1/_2$ mi L 1st Bondsville dam
	$4^3/_4$ mi 2nd Bondsville dam
	$5^1/_4$ mi R dam below MA 181
	$6^1/_2$ mi dam near Jabish Brook

At the MA 9 bridge the current is strong and the water is clean. This type of running continues for a mile to the broken dam at West Ware, where a portage should be made on the right. Four miles of smoothwater follow to Bondsville, with some old bridge abutments about halfway down and a low steel road bridge with a big parking lot $\frac{1}{2}$ mile farther along on the right. Below West Ware the water quality deteriorates considerably.

Because canoeists are not allowed near the 12-foot dam in Bondsville ($4\frac{1}{2}$ mi), take out $\frac{1}{4}$ mile above it at a boat club on the left. This club is accessible from a road along the river. After putting in below the dam, a short paddle leads to a 3-foot dam just below.

The MA 181 bridge (5 mi) is passed, then another dam and a short, easy Class II rapid. The Swift River then winds sluggishly to Jabish Brook ($6\frac{1}{2}$ mi), where a milldam necessitates another easy carry. The river continues for another $1\frac{1}{2}$ miles through pretty country to its confluence with the Ware River. Take out either $\frac{1}{2}$ mile up the Ware River at the MA 181 bridge or $\frac{3}{4}$ mile downstream in Three Rivers ($8\frac{3}{4}$ mi).

QUABOAG RIVER   MA

The Quaboag River flows west from Quaboag Pond in Brookfield to Three Rivers, where it joins with the Ware River to form the Chicopee River. Its upper part provides a good flatwater trip, its middle section from Warren to Blanchardville is one of the best whitewater trips in central Massachusetts, and the lowest part is again smoothwater.

Due to the large lakes in its watershed, the Quaboag holds its water remarkably well, and it is little affected by a single rain or short dry spell. It can always be run to the middle of June and frequently later.

The upper part of the Quaboag was used as a highway by the Indians. During King Philip's War, 1675-76, Brookfield was wiped out, and it was not re-established until 1686, when only one of the original settlers returned.

The Bay Path, which extended across the territory of the Massachusetts Bay Company from Boston to Springfield, followed this valley and crossed the river by fords near West Brookfield and West Brimfield. Today, highways and a railroad follow the valley of the Quaboag.

Quaboag Pond—Warren   9 mi

Description:	Lake, **flatwater,** Class I
Date checked:	1985
Navigable:	Passable at most water levels
Scenery:	Forested, rural
Maps:	USGS East Brookfield, Warren

This is an attractive flatwater trip that can be extended somewhat by beginning on the Brookfield River above Quaboag Pond. The Quaboag flows here in a broad valley in which towns and other built-up areas are for the most part hidden from the river. At the end of this section, the valley narrows, forcing roads, railroads, and towns closer to the river.

Begin from the road along the north shore of Quaboag Pond. The river begins after about a mile of paddling west along the north shore. The 5^1/$_2$-mile paddle from the pond's outlet to West Brookfield can be tedious in a head wind, as the river is fair-sized and leads through marshy meadows. Near West Brookfield the river passes under a railroad bridge and the MA 67 bridge (6^3/$_4$ mi), just below which the outlet from Wickaboag Pond enters from the right. This pond makes an interesting side trip. For those who wish to avoid all rapids, this bridge is a convenient take-out.

The last 2^1/$_4$ miles to Warren have a stronger current and a few riffles. The first real rapid is just below the Old West Brookfield Road bridge (9 mi) at Lucy Stone Park, a good access point.

Warren—Blanchardville   10^1/$_4$ mi

Description:	Quickwater, Class **II, III,** IV
Date checked:	1988, ST
Navigable:	High or medium water: March through May, after fall rains
Scenery:	Forested, settled, town
Maps:	USGS Warren, Palmer
Portage:	2^1/$_2$ mi R dam at West Warren (difficult) 50 yd

This section is often runnable when nearby rivers are not, due to the many lakes and swamps in its headwaters. The scenery is not pleasant, except for the gorge section, but the river offers a wide variety of rapids.

A gauge is located off MA 67 in West Brimfield, 3/4 mile upstream of the Massachusetts Turnpike bridge. A reading of 3.7 is considered the minimum, with 5.5 constituting high water. These readings translate to -0.3 and 1.3 on the gauge at the put-in.

The put-in is at Lucy Stone State Park north of Warren. One and three-quarters miles of intermittent Class II rapids follow to the broken dam above West Warren. **Caution!** Keep to the right, and scout from the right. The canal on the left leads to large tubes which take the river below old walls. This would be a death trap. The far right of the dam is the location of the Mousehole, now collapsed. A channel exists just to the left of the Mousehole over the ruins of the dam. This channel should be scouted. A short rapid under a bridge leads to a pool above the railroad bridge. The rapid below should not be scouted from the bridge, as the tracks have blind curves and the trains move fast. This is the rare case where it is safer to run a Class III-IV rapid blind. Run either side of the center abutment, move to the right side of the left channel, and work your way through the rocks and holes at the end. There is a good recovery pool. A broken dam is next, followed by a rapid around an island. The dam in West Warren offers a difficult carry on the right (2 1/2 mi).

An alternate put-in lies around the corner on the left. The island is best run on the right. The next broken dam is best run to the left of the two remaining stone columns, although it is possible to run the main section of the dam. The river then passes a former outhouse overhanging the river, a sewage plant which increases the volume of the river, and a railroad bridge. The rapid below this bridge (variously known as Railroad Rapids II and Angel's Field) contains large waves at high water, but has an excellent recovery pool. The island below should be run on the right. Catch the right eddy below where the channel around the island rejoins the main channel in order to scout the rapid below.

This is the Devil's Gorge section, which contains three rapids of decreasing difficulty. The first ends in a 3-foot drop, which is difficult to see from above. At low and medium levels a far right approach is preferred, while high water provides a clear run through the center.

The usual take-out is at a picnic area on MA 67 (5¼ mi), but quickwater continues to Blanchardville (10¼ mi).

Blanchardville—Three Rivers   5¼ mi

Description:	**Flatwater,** Class II
Date checked:	1985
Navigable:	Passable whenever ice-free
Scenery:	Forested, towns
Map:	USGS Palmer

The final segment of the Quaboag is almost entirely flat. This stretch, however, is not as attractive as the upper river because of obstructions in the river and the towns along the banks.

The dam at Blanchardville was washed out by the 1955 flood, and only three stone bridge supports remain. A center route is recommended here. The cement blocks and protruding reinforcement rods just below can be avoided because the current is minimal. There are more obstacles at an island, with the right channel and its breached earthen dam more easily navigated than the jumble of steel and concrete at the end of the left channel. The earthen dam, constructed by the Palmer Paving Corporation, is usually washed out in the spring and rebuilt in the low water of summer.

One and a half miles of flatwater follow to Palmer (2 mi). The final 3¼ miles to Three Rivers are also smooth. Because of the rough water created by blasting and dredging below the confluence with the Ware River, a take-out is urged above the first bridge (5¼ mi) in Three Rivers.

SEVEN MILE and BROOKFIELD RIVERS   MA

Spencer—Quaboag Pond   6¹/₄ mi

Description:	Flatwater, quickwater, Class I
Date checked:	1989, RJ
Navigable:	High water: March, April
Scenery:	Forested, settled
Maps:	USGS North Brookfield, East Brookfield

In the early spring, this trip in the headwaters of the Quaboag provides a nice, easy run for two to three hours. At the beginning there are many houses visible from the river, but the farther downstream you travel, the less you see of houses, buildings, and roads. Below East Brookfield the Seven Mile River enters a wide, isolated flood plain and empties into the Brookfield River, which in turn flows into Quaboag Pond.

Put in next to the Pine Grove Cemetery where MA 31 crosses the river north of Spencer. The first 2 miles to the MA 9 bridge are flat and mostly wind through a meadow. Portions of the stream are narrow, but encroaching alders are kept clipped back by canoeists who run it regularly. There are a few beaver dams, which can be run at high water.

As the river passes a shopping center next to the MA 9 bridge (2 mi), the current picks up, and for the next 2 miles there is a mixture of quickwater and occasional Class I rapids to a high bridge over an old dam site in East Brookfield (4 mi). The river here is typically 10 yards wide, and it is shallow with a gravelly bottom.

The remainder of the trip is on flatwater. The Seven Mile River ends at the Brookfield River (4¹/₂ mi). The latter is almost all flatwater from the dam on Lake Lashaway (³/₄ mi upstream). To the left, it flows 1³/₄ miles to Quaboag Pond (6¹/₄ mi).

WESTFIELD RIVER   MA

The Westfield River is one of the principal tributaries of the Connecticut River. It has four important branches: the North Branch (which is also considered the main river); the Middle Branch; and the West Branch, which all meet at Huntington to form the main river, and the Westfield Little River, which enters at Westfield. Additional information about the river can be obtained from the Westfield River Watershed Association, P.O. Box 256, Westfield, MA 01086.

Huntington—Connecticut River   21 mi

Description:	Flatwater, quickwater, Class I, II
Date checked:	1989, JC
Navigable:	Dam-controlled: spring, early summer
Scenery:	Rural, towns
Maps:	USGS Woronoco, Mount Tom, West Springfield, Springfield South
Portages:	1 mi L Texon
	3 mi R Russell
	6 mi R Woronoco

The first dam is 1 mile below Huntington, where the dam at the paper mill can be carried on the left. There are easy rapids in the next 2 miles to the dam at Russell, which should be carried on the right. There are fewer rapids below and several stretches of flatwater in the 3 miles to the dam at Woronoco. This difficult portage is best made on the right bank by taking out at Bull Rock above the pump house, carrying down the highway across the bridge to the left, and dropping down a steep bank through the brush back to the river.

About 2 miles below here the river runs out of the mountains and into a broad valley to meander 4 miles to Westfield. One-quarter mile above the MA 10/202 bridge in Westfield there are three river-wide ledges that are excellent for surfing. It is adjacent to the city ball field, so the put-in and take-out are the same. Below Westfield the river is mainly flatwater. In 1 mile the Westfield Little River enters on the right, and in 2 miles more the river cuts through the low hills north of Proven Mountain into the Connecticut Valley, which it crosses for 6 miles to reach the Connecticut River just south of West Springfield.

WESTFIELD RIVER, North Branch   MA

The North Branch of the Westfield River rises in Windsor in the Hoosac Mountains and flows southeast to Cummington, then south to meet the main Westfield River at Huntington. It provides one of the longest whitewater runs in Massachusetts, a fine run in the spring and even later if the season is wet enough. MA 9 follows the valley from Swift River to West Cummington, so that one can judge the most suitable starting point for the existing water conditions. If the water is high enough, a good place to start is just below Berkshire Snow Basin Ski Area in West Cummington.

Windsor Forest—Cummington   9 mi

Description:	Class I, II
Date checked:	1985
Navigable:	High water: March
Scenery:	Forested, towns
Maps:	USGS Windsor, Worthington

Above West Cummington at Windsor State Forest the river is a rollicking Class II trip in early spring or after a heavy rain. The only problem lies below MA 9. When you see the cemetery on your left, keep to the inside and watch for a small ledge around a left turn. In high water the hydraulic below this ledge is strong enough to keep a boat and paddler. The third MA 9 bridge is Cummington, where the best access is downstream on the right.

Cummington—West Chesterfield   7¹/₂ mi

Description:	Class II, III
Date checked:	1989, EC, CC
Navigable:	High water: March, April
Scenery:	Forested, wild
Maps:	USGS Worthington, Goshen

It is possible to put in at the MA 9 bridge, at the town beach opposite the West Cummington library, or at a rest area on MA 9. This section is popularly referred to as the Pork Barrel, after a former pothole in the river, since filled in. This section offers continuous Class II rapids, with a Class III rapid in every turn. After leaving MA 9, the Swift River enters left and the river turns sharp right. The next 5 miles are isolated. This is a beautiful, wild valley, much of which has been protected by the Nature Conservancy. There are two beautiful waterfalls in this section. About 1/4 mile above West Chesterfield are the remains of an old dam, now totally washed out. This is the first place where a car can reach the river, and it offers a possible take-out. A more popular take-out is below the MA 143 bridge on the right.

West Chesterfield—Knightsville Dam   11 mi

Description:	Class II, III
Date checked:	1985
Navigable:	High water: March, April
Scenery:	Forested, wild
Maps:	USGS Goshen, Westhampton
Portage:	1 mi R Chesterfield Gorge 1/4 mi
	(17½ mi L Knightsville Dam)

If there is enough water here there will be enough water for the rest of the trip. One mile below the bridge the river makes a sharp right turn with a heavy rapid. The beach on the right offers a good lunch spot with a swimming hole below. The beach can also be used as a take-out unless the access road to it is too muddy. About ½ mile below this spot the river turns left with a sharp rapid and enters the West Chesterfield Gorge, which is runnable by experts at certain water levels. **Caution!** Take out on the right bank just above the curve. This may be a difficult maneuver, and it is easy to be swept into the gorge. Be sure to plan the landing carefully.

The West Chesterfield Gorge is a spectacular box canyon between sheer granite cliffs that are topped by tall hemlocks and spruce. At the upper end of the gorge are the remains of a high bridge that carried the old stage road from 1769 to about 1875. Both banks are now owned by the Trustees of Reservations, who have torn down the old houses there to provide a public vista for the gorge. The carry is $1/4$ mile by the road, which follows the right bank downstream. A car is handy for this chore. In low water, one can line down on the left, carry the largest drop, and run the rest of the gorge.

Put in from the road on the right below the gorge. For the next 8 miles the river continues in a steep, narrow valley with heavy rapids for 4 miles. About 200 yards below the gorge there is a heavy rapid through some ledges, which can be dangerous at high water. This can best be run by keeping well to the left and taking advantage of back eddies between the pitches. After about 1 mile of easier rapids the Boulder Patch is reached. **Caution!** Land on the right bank when large white boulders are noticed ahead. The route is intricate and ends in only one usable chute at the finish. Scouting is necessary here as the route may change with the stage of water. The steepest pitch can be lined down or portaged on the right if one prefers not to run it. Not far below here the river passes under a large telephone cable, beyond which there are several very good campsites on the left bank among open pine and hemlock groves. The rapids are easier here and may lull you into a false sense of security. This will be rudely shattered 1 mile below, where there is another steep drop at a right turn. About 2 miles below this rapid the river enters a stillwater gorge that is very spectacular and a fine swimming hole. This is the end of the heavy going, but there are still lively bits for the next 4 miles to the Knightsville Dam. The surroundings are not as attractive here, as flooding by the dam tends to cover the once-pretty farmlands with silt. The old roads are still in use in the dam area, and one from MA 12 just above the dam can be used to take out. Be sure to park well above the water; a rapid increase in the water level above the dam has been known to cover cars parked too close. If conditions are unattractive, the canoeist may prefer to take out about 2 miles below the stillwater gorge, where the old road borders the river on the right.

Knightsville Dam—Huntington   **5 mi**

Description:	Class III
Date checked:	1989, EC, CC
Navigable:	Dam-controlled
Scenery:	Forested, towns
Maps:	USGS Westhampton, Woronoco

This section often has water when the upper section does not. Water releases from the flood control dam aid racers and recreational paddlers alike. Release information may be obtained from the Corps of Engineers.

Put in from the picnic area downstream from the dam, reached from a side road off MA 112 north of MA 66. A low 1– to 2– foot dam may be run in the middle in low water. The rapids continue for 1 mile, then the river turns left and passes through some vertical strata of rock, where a minor gorge is formed. This section contains a 40-foot chute between ledges ending in a deep pool. The next drop is below the pool, a direct drop of 2– to 3–feet, best run on the far right. Next comes this section's most difficult drop. A shallow island in the middle of the river marks the drop. The right side has a large hydraulic and haystacks that can flip a boat at high water. In low water, it is the only viable route. The left side of the island presents a shallow, twisting passage in high water. Careful scouting is recommended for those not familiar with the river.

A short distance below the gorge the Middle Branch enters, and the water volume increases noticeably. In about 1 mile the MA 112 bridge is reached, and just below is a beautiful haystack rapid. Approximately 1/4 mile below, as the river nears MA 112, an old washed-out dam signals the start of the Boulder Patch, which is full of eddies. This is a solid Class III rapid at 1000 cfs.

The West Branch enters at a high railroad bridge. Take out on the right at a picnic area 1/2 mile below.

WESTFIELD RIVER, Middle Branch   MA

The Middle Branch rises in Peru and flows southeasterly to the North Branch 1 mile above the town of Huntington. It is much smaller than the North or West branches and is followed by a road. The stream is continuously rapid, but the water is rarely heavy enough to be dangerous.

Smiths Hollow—Dayville   10 mi

Description:	Class II, III
Date checked:	1989, EC, ST
Navigable:	High water: March, April
Scenery:	Forested
Maps:	USGS Worthington, Chester, Westhampton

To reach the Middle Branch, go north from US 20 on MA 112, cross the West Branch, and take a left onto Basket Road. Follow the latter along the West Branch and then take a road to the right that leads to Dayville.

Put in anywhere along the road that follows the Middle Branch. The gradient is a constant 30 feet per mile. The 6 miles to North Chester are all rapid (Class II-III), with a short gorge in North Chester. There is a gauge on the right abutment of the bridge in the gorge, with 0.0 considered minimum and 4.0 considered high. The next 2 miles to Dayville are also Class II-III rapids. Most people take out in Dayville, because the road to the reservoir is unplowed. If you are lucky enough to run the river when the road is open, 1 mile of harder, Class III rapids leads to the reservoir.

Littleville Dam—North Branch   1 mi

Below the Littleville Dam, 1 mile of Class III rapids leads to the North Branch when releases are made from the dam. Access is from a left turn just before the MA 112 bridge crosses the North Branch.

WESTFIELD RIVER, West Branch   MA

The West Branch of the Westfield is one of the best early spring Class IV runs in New England. The valley from Becket to Chester is isolated, marked only with beautiful stone-arch railroad bridges and the mill and bridge at Bancroft. More than one paddler has been reduced to dragging a boat down the tracks following a mishap.

Becket—Bancroft   3¹/₂ mi

Description:	Class IV
Date checked:	1989, ST, EC
Navigable:	High water: spring
Scenery:	Wild, forested
Map:	USGS Becket
Portage:	3 mi R double ledge (optional)
	3¹/₂ mi L dam (recommended)

Put in on the left bank off a side street just below the main bridge in Becket. The run is continuous Class IV. Approximately 2¹/₂ miles into the trip, watch for a steep bank on the right and a sharp left turn. This marks the Stain of Shame rapids, which involve tight maneuvering in heavy waves, with broaching possibilities. After a short pool, there is a long standing-wave rapid that ends in a left turn and a ledge under the railroad bridge. Shortly below comes the double ledge. Scout left, portage right. A stream enters on the left between the ledges. The Bancroft Dam follows. Although this has been run, the spikes and debris there suggest easy portage on the left. The Bancroft bridge is just below.

Bancroft—Chester   6 mi

Description:	Class IV
Date checked:	1989, ST, EC
Navigable:	High water: spring
Scenery:	Wild, forested
Maps:	USGS Becket, Chester

This section is, on average, not as difficult as the upper section, but there are two noteworthy rapids. Watch for an island with the main channel on the right. This should be scouted, as the current is deflected by a large boulder, resulting in difficult cross currents at a drop. Class III rapids follow the drop. The next spot to scout is the gorge. A double ledge in the gorge creates large holes at high water. A small difference in the height of the river up above translates to a large difference here. A road runs along the river for the last mile to Chester.

Chester—Huntington   6 mi

Description:	Class II, III
Date checked:	1989, EC
Navigable:	High water: spring
Scenery:	Rural, towns
Maps:	USGS Chester, Blanford, Woronoco

At Chester the river is joined by Walker Brook, which adds considerably to its volume. After passing under a railroad bridge about 3 miles below Chester, there is a fine long rapid, steep but easily run at moderate water stages. The two broken dams above Huntington are being completely washed out, exposing ledge drops where the dams were constructed. Both are runnable and can be scouted from the road on the north side of the river.

WALKER BROOK   MA

Walker Brook is a small tributary of the West Branch which has increased in popularity in recent years. It is extremely steep and narrow. In places, it is too narrow to make an eddy turn. Eddies are scarce.

US 20—Chester   3$\frac{1}{2}$ mi

Description:	Class **IV**, V
Date checked:	1989, JM
Navigable:	High water: early spring
Map:	USGS Chester

Put in anywhere on US 20 as it follows the river. A suggested put-in is 3¹/₂ miles west of Chester. The first mile is Class V. One-half mile below this section is a 200-yard Class V rapid, considered the hardest on the river. A put-in below here will result in steep, narrow, technical Class IV water for the remaining 2 miles to Chester. You will not see the scenery along this stretch.

FARMINGTON RIVER   MA, CT

The Farmington River is a gem. It offers something for every canoeist—pleasant flatwater stretches, Class I-II training spots, Class II-III training spots, Class III-IV rapids, and training sites for slalom racers. What makes the Farmington unique is the opportunities provided for summer paddling. Tarriffville Gorge always has sufficient water to paddle; the rapids below Riverton, Satan's Kingdom, and Collinsville can often be run during the summer. Dam releases provide Class III-IV rapids for experts and a Class II section in the upper area of the river. The water quality is clear but not potable.

The Farmington River Watershed Association, 749 Hopmeadow St., Simsbury, CT 06070, is an excellent source of river information. Their book *The Farmington River Guide* ($5 postpaid) is an excellent source of river descriptions, information on the wildlife and geology of the valley, and information on the trails, parks, and forests. The FRWA (203-658-4442) can be contacted after business hours on Thursdays for river-level information.

MA 8—Below New Boston   7 mi

Description:	Class II, III-IV
Date checked:	1989, KH, ST
Navigable:	High to medium water: March, April, annual drawdown of Otis Reservoir
Scenery:	Forested, town
Maps:	USGS Otis, Tolland Center

This run is broken into three parts. The 2 miles from the bridge adjacent to MA 8 to the green bridge leading to Tolland State Forest are Class II and provide a good warm-up for the more difficult rapids below. The 3 miles from the bridge to the MA 8/57 bridge in New Boston are Class III-IV, and the 2 miles to the impoundment area for Colebrook dam are Class II, ending in a series of Class III rapids. The run can be made in the early spring or in October with the aid of water releases from Otis Reservoir. The rapids are continuous Class III-IV below the Tolland State Park bridge. The entire run is paralleled by MA 8, which facilitates scouting or impromptu take-outs.

There is a gauge on a side-road bridge between the two MA 8 bridges south of New Boston. The minimum level is 3.6, with 4.0 required for a fluid run. The fall releases from Otis Reservoir result in a gauge level in this range, although the addition of natural runoff provides the potential for a higher level. The middle 3 miles are Class IV at levels above 5 feet, with no rests.

Put in at a side-road bridge 2 miles above the Tolland State Park bridge. Flatwater leads to an easy Class II rapid, then a harder, longer Class II stretch. Eddies and surfing opportunities abound. A pool by a campground ends at a rock dam, which is easily run. Beaver dams are often found in the next section. More Class II rapids lead to the Tolland State Park bridge (2 mi), the site of an annual slalom race.

The Race Course Rapid marks the beginning of the more difficult section. A 3-foot drop follows in a straight section. The next rapid is long and technical, and involves moving from right to left and back right. The end of this rapid is marked by an undercut eddy on the right. Ferry left and scout Decoration Rock Rapid (Class IV).

Decoration Rock (2½ mi) changes from year to year. Recent highway construction on the right bank has resulted in the potential for double broaching. Carry on the left if you're unsure of your abilities. This is the most dangerous spot on the river.

Continuous Class III-IV rapids continue for the next 2 miles. A small bridge (4½ mi) followed by a rapid in a right turn warns of the approach to the Washing Machine (a.k.a. Corkscrew). Take out on the right following the right turn and walk down MA 8 to scout.

Below New Boston (5 mi) the Farmington is generally Class II. Access at the New Boston bridge is a problem. Although the AMC has been arranging a take-out at the Legion in recent years, this could change. It is suggested that paddlers complete the run to the Bear's Den.

From the MA 8 bridge there are 2 miles of rapids mixed with flatwater that extend to the next MA 8 bridge. The gauge is passed along the way, downstream on the left abutment at a small bridge. One-quarter mile below the lower MA 8 bridge lies a Class III rapid called the Bear's Den. Scout from the right bank. If you can't make an eddy turn don't try this rapid. The best take-out is below this rapid (7 mi).

Below New Boston—Hogback Dam   6 mi

Map:	USGS Winsted

This description is for information only. It is not anticipated that anyone will wish to make the necessary portages. The river below the Bear's Den is mildly riffled until it enters the backwater of Colebrook Dam (³/₄ mi). The carries around Colebrook Dam and Hogback Dam are on the right and posted signs must be followed.

Hogback Dam—Collinsville   15¹/₄ mi

Description:	Flatwater, quickwater, **Class I-II**
Date checked:	1989, KH, ST
Navigable:	High to medium water: March, April, annual drawdown of Otis Reservoir
Scenery:	Forested, rural, settled
Maps:	USGS Winsted, New Hartford, Collinsville
Portage:	(15¹/₄ mi R first dam in Collinsville)

The upper part of this section from Hogback Dam to Satan's Kingdom is a beautiful run of mixed quickwater and Class I-II rapids between hills and woods. The upper section is largely bordered by state land. The nature of this section is dependent upon rainfall and the discharge from Hogback Dam, with 150 cfs the minimum level; 250 cfs is preferred. In summer and fall the river provides many miles of easy rapids mixed with flatwater. The river can be dangerous in high water, as it flows around shoreside vegetation.

Put in just below Hogback Dam at a little turnout on Hogback

Road, which leaves CT 20 about ¹/₂ mile north of Riverton. The run to Riverton consists of 1³/₄ miles of Class II rapids. A state picnic area opposite the Hitchcock Chair Factory in Riverton provides another convenient access to the river.

The Still River enters on the right in 1/4 mile. Class II rapids alternate with flatwater until you reach a stand of tall pines on a high bank with a fence on the left. High Bank Rapids is the most difficult in this stretch, with big rocks in its midst. After the CT 181 bridge (6 mi), the river broadens out with occasional narrow areas that produce riffles. The CT 219 bridge is next. The high US 44 bridge marks the entrance to Satan's Kingdom. There is a good take-out on the right 75 yards above the bridge.

There is a small set of rapids under US 44 followed by a short section of flatwater to the big drop in Satan's Kingdom. Scout left. This drop is best run at medium levels, although it is runnable on the right in the summer. In high water this becomes a difficult Class III rapid and must be run with caution. The drop is steep and the channel twists due to several large, partially submerged boulders midstream. The river forks in a mile. Both forks are runnable. Watch out for tubers in this section. Rooster Tail Rapid (II+) is in this section.

Soon US 44 comes into view on the left bank, and the rest of the run to Collinsville Dam is intermittent, easy Class II rapids up to a high silver bridge, where the river becomes flat for the remaining mile to the dam. Keep right in this area when waterskiers are present. Land on the left for the take-out and on the right to continue beyond the dam.

Description:	Class II
Date checked:	1989, KH, ST
Navigable:	Sufficient flow most of the year. Too low during drought.
Scenery:	Forested, town
Map:	USGS Collinsville
Portage:	1 mi R second dam in Collinsville

There is a Class III rapid immediately below the first dam in Collinsville, followed by flatwater. Due to the difficulty of the put-in and the necessity to portage the second dam in Collinsville, most paddlers will put in at a turn-off on CT 179. From this point the Farmington has a series of complex but moderate drops which are excellent for training beginners. The initial rapid, Crystal Rapid, should be run on the left. The stone snake wall on the left, marks the entrance to the final two rapids, which are the most difficult of the trip. The CT 4 bridge is just below the last rapid in this section (4^1/$_4$ mi), which should be exited on the right. A possible take-out is ^{1}/$_4$ mile below the CT 4 bridge on the right on River Road.

The river then flows through Unionville. Opposite Apricots Restaurant, which offers riverside dining in the summer, the river becomes very ledgy, and in ^{1}/$_2$ mile, reaches Boateater Rapid. The river comes together and flows against the right bank, but the boulder for which the rapid was named has been moved by floods. Take out below at a town park above the railroad bridge, which can be found by driving east on CT 4 and turning right at a convenience store just before a railroad overpass.

Boateater Rapid—Tarriffville Park   **18 mi**

Description:	Flatwater
Date checked:	1989, KH
Navigable:	Navigable at all water levels
Scenery:	Rural, towns
Maps:	USGS Avon, New Britain, Tarriffville
Portage:	2^1/$_2$ mi L dam at Farmington

The railroad bridge at the put-in should be run to the left of the left abutment. The river then flattens out and flows through a large gravel pit. The Pequabuck River (2 mi) enters from the right where the river turns left. Portage the dam (2^1/$_2$ mi) on the left. There is a take-out on the left at the CT 4 bridge in Farmington.

The river below Farmington is very pleasant, providing good views of Talcott Mountain. It is 6 miles from the CT 4 bridge to the US 44/CT 10 bridge and additional 7^1/$_2$ miles to the CT 315 bridge

(16¹/₂ mi) north of Simsbury. The latter is the seventh bridge, counting the CT 4 bridge at Farmington and both bridges at Drakes Hill Road at Simsbury, and it is the recommended take-out for flatwater paddlers. One-and-a-half miles below (18 mi), and after a bend in the river, high bridge abutments are seen. All flatwater paddlers should take out on the right here, as just below lies Tarriffville Gorge. This take-out can be reached by following the main street in Tarriffville to the end and turning right down a gravel road to Tarriffville Park.

Tarriffville Park—CT 187   1¹/₂ mi

Description:	Class **II-III**, IV
Date checked:	1989, KH, ST
Navigable:	High water: spring, after heavy rains. Over 3.5 on gauge
	Medium water: late spring. 2.3–3.5 on gauge
	Low/medium water: normal summer level. 1.4–2.2 on gauge
	Low water: during Stanley Works shutdown, two weeks in summer
Scenery:	Forested, settled
Map:	USGS Tarriffville
Portage:	1 mi L Spoonville Dam (optional)

The gauge is difficult to find and read prior to putting in, so it is suggested that the Connecticut Chapter AMC hotline (203-582-6978) be utilized for information regarding river levels. High water results in Class IV conditions, with large waves and holes. Playing is largely confined to Cathy's Wave. Medium levels find the classic play hole largely washed out, but there are other surfing opportunities. The run is Class III at these levels, with the dam considered Class III-IV. At low to medium water you find the most surfing opportunities. Low water occurs when the Stanley Works, which owns the water rights to Rainbow Dam downstream, shuts down. The river is Class II at this level, and the holes are difficult to escape. This section is rarely too low to paddle, although the run above the Bridge Abutments Rapid is scratchy at low water. The renovations to the Sewer Treatment Plant in Bristol have greatly improved water quality in the area, especially at low water.

To reach the put-in, follow the main street off CT 189 to the end and turn right down a gravel road. Small ledges greet the paddler shortly below. These ledges can be run almost anywhere and provide an introduction to surfing. A small island is passed following the CT 189 bridge (1/4 mi), followed by a surfing wave above a factory on the right; this wave is best at normal summer levels. Cathy's Wave, which is best at high water, is formed by the concrete retaining wall at the factory. The gauge is found below this area, on the right bank. Lower Brown Ledge follows, with good surfing waves.

Bridge Abutment Rapids are next. It is possible to carry up from the dead end on river left to a point above this rapid. Two sets of abutments are present. At normal summer levels the best route is to the right of the abutments, enjoying many right eddies. A safer route at high water leads between the sets of abutments.

The next drop should be scouted from the left bank by novices. This drop, known as Sandy Beach Rapid, is riddled with holes. The clearest route is left; the most fun, down the middle. The beach follows on the left. This area is at its prime in low to medium water, when the run is Class II-III. This is the area where paddlers advance their skills: The Lower Hole, which is the most benign, is followed by a good pool; and the Top and Upper Holes are also interesting. Try to avoid surfing the Pencil Sharpener on the right as the river is too shallow in this area. Access to this area is gained by crossing the river on CT 187 north, turning right on Spoonville Road, and bearing right twice to a dead end.

The rapid following the beach is best run as a series of left eddy turns at normal summer levels. High water opens up other possibilities.

Spoonville Dam (1 mi) follows a flatwater stretch. Scout or portage left. The hazard is a piece of the dam (Car Rock) that has been deposited downstream. Avoid the left side of the chute because of debris on the bottom; the right side has a nasty hole. The best run at normal summer levels is right center, through the largest wave, heading right. At levels around 3.0 on the gauge, this wave forms a hole, so the chute left center should be run. Then execute a mandatory left eddy above Car Rock, followed by a ferry move across the current to the large right eddy below the dam. Form your own decision.

The Farmington then goes sharply left around an island, then sharply right. The best move is to make this left eddy and surf across Typewriter Wave to below the island. The river then enters a slalom training area. A low dam on the right forms dangerous hydraulics and should be avoided. The rest of the run to CT 187 (1 1/2 mi) is through shallow water.

CT 187—Connecticut River   11 1/2 mi

Description:	**Flatwater,** Class II
Date checked:	1989, KH
Navigable:	Navigable at all water levels
Scenery:	Rural, towns
Maps:	USGS Tarriffville, Windsor Locks, Hartford North
Portage:	3 1/2 mi R Rainbow Dam

River access here is under the CT 187 bridge. Go south on CT 187/189 to the Tarriffville Road exit, turn left at the exit, take the next left to the end, going down a rough road. Below CT 187 the river continues shallow and broad until reaching the backwater from Rainbow Dam (3 1/2 mi). The state access is on the left bank about 1/2 mile upstream of the dam, and the portage is on the right about thirty yards upstream of the dam. On the left side of the dam there is a fish ladder that is providing for re-entry of salmon into the river.

The water level for the rest of the river is dependent on the Rainbow Dam. It is 1 1/2 miles to the CT 75 bridge (5 1/4 mi) in Poquonock, below which are 1/4 mile of Class II rapids. The river becomes flat and flows under I-91 (7 3/4 mi) and the CT 159 bridge, where there is a good take-out (10-1/4 mi). There then remains 1 1/4 miles of flatwater to the Connecticut River (11 1/2 mi).

SANDY BROOK   CT

Sandy Brook rises near South Sandisfield, MA, and flows southeastward into Connecticut. Above the CT 8 bridge the Sandy provides one of the best whitewater runs in Connecticut. The rapids moderate below CT 8. There are no major lakes or reservoirs in its headwaters, so it is rarely runnable.

Campbell Road Bridge—CT 8   4 mi

Description:	Class IV
Date checked:	1989, KH
Navigable:	High water: March, early April, after heavy rain
Scenery:	Forested
Maps:	USGS Tolland Center, Winstead

The former gauge at the CT 8 bridge has been destroyed by construction. There is a new gauge on a rock downstream from this bridge on the left. It is estimated that a reading of 0.0 is required for a smooth run, with 1.0 representing high water.

To reach the put-in, turn west off CT 8 onto Sandy Brook Road. The road follows the river closely and crosses it several times, facilitating scouting, putting in, and taking out. A start can be made wherever desired, with one possibility being the Campbell Road bridge about 4 miles upstream from CT 8.

Rapids begin immediately, and a couple of small ledge drops are followed by a 4-foot ledge best run in the center. This drop should be scouted. Shortly below is the Block Rapid, where a series of ledges and large holes finish with an extremely tight drop around either side of a rock outcropping. Scout this drop, also.

A bridge 3/4 mile downstream offers a put-in for those who do not want the difficulties above. What follows is extremely steep and narrow, with continuous Class IV rapids. The water is rarely heavy enough to be intimidating, but fallen trees present a frequent and formidable hazard throughout this run. Many rapids may require scouting, if only because the large rocks, tight turns, and steep gradient make it difficult to boat scout. This entire run approaches Class V in high water.

CT 8—Riverton 2 mi

Description:	Class II-III
Date checked:	1989, KH
Navigable:	High water: March, April, after heavy rain
Scenery:	Forested, pasture
Map:	USGS Winstead

This section of Sandy Brook is still rapid, but is not nearly as difficult as the upper stretch. The river is wider, with fallen trees less of a hazard. This section can be run when the upper section is too low.

Put in from the CT 8 bridge. Rapids follow for 1 mile and are generally Class II-III. Once the river empties into the Still River, the rapids are even easier Class II to the town of Riverton.

NEPAUG RIVER CT

The Nepaug rises in New Hartford and flows east through Tunxis State Forest into the Nepaug Reservoir. Above CT 219 this crystal-clear sandy-bottom stream is shallow, steep, and full of blowdowns. The river is runnable from Dings Road to the last US 202 bridge above the reservoir.

Ding Road—US 202 4 mi

Description:	Class I-II
Date checked:	1989, KH
Navigable:	High water: March, early April, after heavy rain
Scenery:	Forested, pasture

There is a gauge 1/3 mile east of the US 202 take-out. The Nepaug is barely runnable at a reading of 1.0. For a fluid run, 1.75 is suggested. To reach the put-in take Carpenter Road to Dings Road off US 202 in New Hartford. The river crosses Carpenter Road and US 202 several times.

The river meanders through an old pasture and then crosses US 202 at an easy rapid ($^1/_4$ mi). Below this crossing there is another Class II pitch, ending just before the second US 202 bridge. The remainder is Class I through deep woods, with occasional blowdowns. Do not proceed below the last US 202 bridge, for this is owned by the MDC and is posted.

HUBBARD BROOK   MA

Hubbard Brook rises in West Granville, MA, east of the Upper Farmington, and flows south into the Barkhamsted Reservoir in Connecticut. The river is crystal-clear, ledgy, technical, and steep. With a gradient of 60 to 300 feet per mile, it is by far the steepest river described in this guide. All rapids are runnable by experts under certain conditions, but everyone should decide for him or herself. The Barkhamsted Reservoir provides drinking water for the Hartford area.

MA 57—CT 20   6 mi

Description:	Class **IV**-V
Date checked:	1989, KH, JM
Navigable:	High water: March, April, after heavy rain
Scenery:	Forested
Portages:	Nosepin, The Big One, Outer Limits, others

Put in at MA 57, 7 miles east of New Boston or $^1/_2$ mile west of the entrance to Granville State Park. The river to Granville State Park is generally Class III-IV with a difficult pitch just before the park bridge. Below the bridge, an 8-foot boulder on the left marks 7-Foot Falls. If you're having trouble so far, take out on the right. The rapids get significantly harder.

The next drop after leaving the camping area is Nosepin. It is suggested that you portage this rapid, although it is runnable. Scout it. Class IV rapids continue to a river-wide horizon line. Bump and Grind Slide should be scouted. Following are a series of 5- and 6-foot ledges leading to The Big One. Most will portage this rapid. The

river gets even steeper below here, culminating in Outer Limits, a
$1/2$-mile rapid with a gradient of 300 feet per mile. The take-out is at
the gauge pool approximately $1/2$ mile from CT 20 on a dirt road on
the east side. The suggested gauge readings for this river are 3.5 to
4.3.

HOCKANUM RIVER   CT

The Hockanum River rises from Shenipsit Lake on the borders of
Ellington, Tolland, and Vernon, and flows westward to the
Connecticut River in East Hartford. The watershed is heavily
developed and it is a notorious flash river, rising and falling quickly.
Once regarded as one of Connecticut's most polluted, the "Hock"
has made remarkable progress, although there is ample opportunity
for improvement. Local river advocates have been lobbying for a
linear park along the river, and a popular annual canoe race was
established in 1977 to draw attention to the river. Despite passing
through the heart of Manchester, many stretches remain very scenic.
Remnants of historic mill sites can still be found.

Rockville—Talcottville   7 mi

Description:	Quickwater
Date checked:	1989, SG
Navigable:	High water: March, April, after heavy rain
Scenery:	Rural, suburban
Maps:	USGS Rockville, Manchester

This is a very small stream, often flowing through backyards, and
can only be run during very high water. There are three dams in the
town of Rockville. According to older accounts, the first practical
put-in is at West Street, but this upper stretch has not been scouted in
recent years (try at your own risk). A better bet may be Dart Hill
Road, easily accessed west of CT 83. The 2 miles to I-84 are
winding, flat, and quickwater, with a lot of brush and some shopping
carts. Shortly below I-84 the Tankerhossen River enters in the
middle of a mini-golf course, quickly followed by a footbridge,

which is the starting point for the annual Hockanum River Canoe Race.

Talcottville—Powder Mill Plaza, East Hartford   6½ mi

Description:	**Quickwater,** Class I-II
Date checked:	1989, SG
Navigable:	High water: March, April, after heavy rain
Scenery:	Urban, suburban, forested
Map:	USGS Manchester
Portages:	1¼ mi L Union Pond dam 50 yd
	(6½ mi R Powder Mill dam 20 yd)

This stretch is the race course. It is a bigger stream than above, but still only runnable after rains (except below CT 44). The first mile is a pleasant meadow stream with quick current, running between I-84 and CT 83. After a high exit-ramp bridge, the river descends a series of ledges that can be Class II or III (highwater). Scouting is advisable and can be accomplished via the "Cadkey" parking lot (across from an old brick mill) off CT 83, Oakland Street. The rapids can be portaged on the left bank.

After the rapids comes the large, yet shallow, Union Pond. Portage the dam to the left. A new Union Street bridge is under construction as of this writing. If the river is inaccessible between the dam and bridge, cross the street and put in below. The next 2 miles are winding quickwater with some tight turns. They can be negotiated by novices but are challenging enough to hold the interest of veterans. The river passes under several bridges and the scenery slowly changes to residential. Shortly after the Hilliard Street bridge (the fourth bridge), the river enters a low, flat stretch with many bends that give way to the CT 44 bridge and an expansive marsh still known as Laurel Lake. Pardon the high-rise landfill to the left. The USGS map still shows a lake, but the dam is breached and the stream winds around cattails. The old Powder Mill Dam is reached about ten minutes below the triple I-84 bridges. Portage on the right behind McDonald's and a tall concrete wall. This is the usual take-out point. New fences behind the Powder Mill Shopping Plaza may require arrangements for access.

Powder Mill Plaza—Connecticut River   5¹/₂ mi

Description:	Flatwater, tidal
Date checked:	1989, SG
Navigable:	Medium water: may be scratchy in riffles and shallow in muddy areas
Scenery:	Urban
Maps:	USGS Manchester, Hartford North
Portages:	1 mi R Scotland Rd. dam 10 yd
	1¹/₄ mi L Church St. dam 10 yd
	1¹/₂ mi L dam below Church St. 10 yd

This stretch is mostly dam-impoundment or tidewater from the Connecticut River and, as such, can be canoed during most seasons. There is not much to recommend it except for the paddler intent on making a headwater-to-mouth trip. The charm of the middle river gives way to urban clutter, although the last stretch that passes through the Connecticut River floodplain may be mildly scenic.

Portage or put in on the right bank. Within 1 mile a shallow millpond is reached behind the high school. The new Scotland Road bridge is around the corner; approach to the right. There is a 15-foot dam shortly after the bridge; portage on the right very close to the spillway. Caution should be exercised in very high water. A suitable parking place is adjacent. Two more dams follow in close succession. They can be carried in one portage (about 1,000 ft) behind the brick mill down Church Street, or paddled and portaged individually (scout first). The first portage is to the right (easy), the second is to the left (moderate), followed by a series of ledges runnable in highwater, and the third is to the left (difficult). The lower dam is followed by a short riffle that would be scratchy in low water. After 3 miles of flatwater, the stream opens into a large pond created by removal of highway fill. In another 1¹/₂ miles, the river passes a sewage treatment plant, flows through a dike, and joins the Connecticut River under the shadow of the old Charter Oak Bridge (planned for demolition). Best take-out spots are on the Connecticut River: there is a boat launch upstream on the East Hartford side and one slightly upstream across the river at Charter Oak Landing in Hartford.

COGINCHAUG RIVER   CT

The Coginchaug River begins in northern Guilford and flows north through Durham, Middlefield, and Middletown before flowing into the Mattabassett River about 1/2 mile upstream of that stream's confluence with the Connecticut. The river from Myer Huber Pond to Meetinghouse Hill Road is very small. From Meetinghouse Hill Road to Durham Road (CT 157), it is swampy and probably runnable at highwater, but possibly littered with a lot of deadfalls. (Not scouted.) Durham Road is a good put-in, as is the Strickland Road Bridge, about 1 mile farther down the river. The numerous portages and the landfill should not scare away the adventurous. It is still a worthwhile trip.

CT 157—CT 66   5-3/4 mi

Description:	Flatwater, quickwater, Class I-II
Date checked:	1989, SG
Navigable:	High water: March, April, after heavy rain
Scenery:	Forested, rural, urban
Maps:	USGS Durham, Middletown
Portages:	2¼ mi L dam/falls at Rockfall 135 yd
	2½ mi R dam at Rockfall 20 yd
	2¾ mi R dam at Rockfall 10 yd
	3 mi L dam at Rogers Manuf. Co. 7 yd
	4¼ mi R dam at Spring St. 125 yd
	4¾ mi R dam at Starr Mill 20 yd

The first 1½ miles flow through scenic, undisturbed swampland, passing the Strickland Road bridge at 1 mile. At 2¼ miles a small stone dam is encountered in front of a bridge. Pull out on the left and scout across the road, which is part of the Wadsworth Falls State Park. Shortly below the dam are the Wadsworth Falls, one of the state's most impressive waterfalls. There is no good portage for the falls, so the dam and falls are best carried as one. Follow the stairs to left of the falls. Around the corner below the falls is a second dam with an easy portage via a right-bank trail. Under the railroad bridge and around another bend is a third dam, which can be easily portaged on either side, but the right (state park) side is recommended to avoid private property. A fourth dam, at Rogers Manufacturing Co. (easily missed on a topographical map), is a short distance below. There is no good portage. At moderate water levels, canoes can be lined down the 8-foot concrete spillway to the right, which tends to be dry. At high levels, take out at the forebay to the left and lower your canoes to each other by crawling down broken concrete alongside the factory building (moderately difficult). It is best to scout on the left. Below the dam enter the main portion of the state park and ride quickwater under a new, wooden bridge, CT 157, and soon reach another millpond. A thick growth of thorns hinders a portage on the left. The recommended carry is on the right side close to the spillway. Carry to the street, turn left, and put in upstream of the bridge in front of the factory. After 1/2 mile of residential area, the Starr Millpond is reached (fifth and last dam). It is best portaged via a fishing trail to the right about 25 feet above the dam. The path leads directly below the 13-foot dam, but if the downed elm tree still blocks the river below the nearby abandoned bridge, it may be best to carry beyond the obstruction. The next 1/2 mile to Washington Street is mostly quickwater with a series of standing waves in the last straightaway. Behind an apartment building there is a breached dam that is easily seen in advance. Although the breach is no problem, the downstream portion is braided, and the best route requires a 180-degree turn to the left at the breach. Whitewater novices should scout.

CT 66—Mouth   2¹/₂ mi

Description:	Quickwater, mostly tidal
Navigable:	High flows: recommended for non-tidal portion
Scenery:	Urban, extensive floodplain swamp/marsh complex

In the first 3/4 mile you will paddle behind Palmer Field and then pass under an abandoned steel bridge, the new CT 72 bridge, and the old stone CT 72 bridge in rapid succession. During normal flows, the head-of-tide will be encountered below the riffle under the last bridge. When this river is runnable, however, the Connecticut River may be in freshet and backed up to Palmer Field. If you can ignore some trash, power lines, and a few houses, the swamp below is scenic and full of wildlife. The Mattabassett is joined in the middle of an expansive tidal marsh under a railroad bridge. Hook to the right around the insulting landfill and paddle another ³/₄ mile toward the Connecticut River. A take-out point at the end of a dirt road between the last railroad bridge and the CT 9 bridge can be reached via Alfredo's Riverside Restaurant. Another take-out option is Harborpark (Middletown's riverfront park), 1 mile downstream on the Connecticut.

SALMON RIVER SYSTEM   CT

For many people, the whitewater season begins on the Salmon River, which flows into the Connecticut River near East Haddam. Runs on the upper part of the river usually begin on the Blackledge or Jeremy rivers, the two small streams that combine to form the Salmon. A large portion of the routes described here pass through the Salmon River State Forest. This is a heavily fished trout stream, and canoeing is not advised on weekends from Opening Day (third Saturday in April) to early May.

Just upstream from the CT 16 bridge is the covered Comstock Bridge. On the downstream side of the right abutment there is an iron ring. The river is passable when it is within two feet of the iron ring.

BLACKLEDGE RIVER

West Road—CT 66   2³/₄ mi

Description:	Quickwater, Class I-II
Date checked:	1989, SG
Navigable:	High water: February, early March
Scenery:	Forested
Map:	USGS Marlborough
Portage:	1¹/₂ mi L dam 20 yd

Begin north of the center of Marlborough at the bridge on West Road, just east of the intersection with Jones Hollow Road. The river here is small as it flows through a marsh. The stretch down to Parker Road is advised only for the adventurous who are prepared to tangle with swamp and beaver dams.

After 50 yards of bushes, the stream is channeled through a gravel pit for $1/4$ mile. Quickwater continues as the valley narrows beyond the gravel pit and the stream enters the woods where bushes occasionally crowd the channel. There are some Class II rapids at an s turn above a small pond where a dam must be portaged. The dam is in a private back yard, so be courteous. Immediately below the dam is the Parker Road bridge, reached through Hebron from the east. This is an alternate put-in. Below the dam ($1^{1}/2$ mi) the river flows through a very attractive wooded valley with few obstructions. There are intermittent Class I and II rapids for $1^{1}/4$ miles to the CT 66 bridge ($2^{3}/4$ mi).

BLACKLEDGE and SALMON RIVERS   CT

This is the more frequently used approach to the Salmon River. The rapids are easier than those on the Jeremy. The most commonly used access to the river is at the Hartford Road bridge southeast of Marlborough.

CT 66—CT 16 $8^{1}/4$ mi

Description:	Quickwater, Class I-**II**
Date checked:	1989, SG
Navigable:	High water: from CT 66, February, early March
	Medium water: from Hartford Rd., late March, after heavy rain
Scenery:	Forested, rural
Maps:	USGS Marlborough, Moodus

In high water this stream can be run from the CT 66 bridge northeast of Marlborough. The first $3^{1}/4$ miles are easy and can be run with little difficulty. The stream is narrow as it passes through a pretty area of woods and pasture. Be alert for fallen trees.

The most common put-in is beside the Hartford Road bridge just above the CT 2 highway bridge. For $2^1/2$ miles past the River Road bridge ($5^1/4$ mi), which provides an alternate access, the river is quickwater to the confluence with the Jeremy River.

Below the confluence ($5^3/4$ mi) there are continuous Class II rapids, easier in high water than in medium. A popular take-out is on River Road beside a handicap-access ramp ($7^1/2$ mi). This whole area is extremely beautiful, with state land on both sides. Scout the washed-out dam ($7^3/4$ mi) below the ramp from the right. The clearest passage is on the right, but others are possible. Rapids continue for $1/2$ mile to the covered bridge, where there is a good take-out, with parking, on the right. If you are willing to run the old dam this is a much better take-out than the handicap-access ramp.

JEREMY AND SALMON RIVERS   CT

Greyville Park—CT 16 $7^1/4$ mi

Description:	Quickwater, Class I-II
Date checked:	1989, SG
Navigable:	High water: February, early March
	Medium water: late March
Scenery:	Forested, rural, towns
Maps:	USGS Colchester, Moodus
Portage:	$3^1/2$ mi L dam at North Westchester 20 yd

Park in Greyville Park in Hebron, off Greyville Road, which connects westward with CT 85. Put in below the falls on Raymond Brook and paddle or line 100 feet to the confluence with the Jeremy. The first 2 miles are recommended only for the adventurous. Watch for downed trees. The first mile to Judd Brook is mostly flat and swampy, while the current quickens during the next mile to Hartford Road (2 mi).

The Hartford Road bridge provides a better put-in. The bridge is reached by turning right at the north end of CT 149. There is limited parking at the bridge. Flatwater is followed by Class II rapids below the CT 2 bridge ($2^1/4$ mi), which are continuous for $1^1/4$ miles to the bridge in North Westchester. There is a small millpond above a dam, which must be portaged on the left. An alternate portage is to take out on the right above a small bridge, carry around the dam and mill, cross the river, and put in on the left bank. The right bank has been posted against trespassing.

Below the dam (3^1/$_2$ mi) Class II rapids continue to the confluence with the Blackledge River (4^3/$_4$ mi).

CT 16—Connecticut River   8^1/$_4$ mi

Description:	Flatwater, **quickwater,** Class I; tidal
Date checked:	1989, SG
Navigable:	High or medium water: February, March, after heavy rain
Scenery:	Forested, towns
Maps:	USGS Moodus, Deep River
Portage:	3^1/$_2$ mi L Leesville Dam

Below the covered bridge next to CT 16, the Salmon River is less steep than above, but still contains rapids and requires a good runoff. Put in either below the covered bridge on the right or at the picnic area on the left, downstream of the CT 16 bridge on Gulf Road. To the left are two imprinting ponds, where salmon smolts are acclimated to the stream prior to being released into the river to swim to the sea and thereby restore the salmon run. Downstream, below Leesville Dam, the first salmon caught on rod and reel within Connecticut during this century was taken in 1977. The dam (3^1/$_2$ mi) is approached after an s turn and an overhead cable designating the upper limit to a no fishing area in the pond. The 12-foot dam is 600 feet below. Approach to the left and tuck into a marshy inlet along the riprap about 50 feet upstream of the fish ladder. There is a small parking lot about 300 feet south where cars can be left. Paddlers continuing downstream can put in behind the fish ladder. The fish ladder is used to trap returning adult salmon. Information about the salmon restoration program is posted on a bulletin board from April to November.

One-and-three-quarters miles below CT 151 (3^3/$_4$ mi), the river enters Salmon Cove (5^1/$_2$ mi), a tidal inlet on the Connecticut River.

You can take out on the main river at the Salmon River boat-launching area on the left (7^1/$_2$ mi) or ^{3}/$_4$ mile farther at the parking area by the Goodspeed Opera House on the left, just past the CT 82 bridge (8^1/$_4$ mi) over the Connecticut River.

EIGHT MILE RIVER   CT

This small, whitewater stream flows through Devil's Hopyard State Park in East Haddam to Hamburg Cove on the Connecticut River in Lyme. North of CT 82 it flows through hemlocks and hardwoods in a narrow valley. The lower part is a mixture of fields, forests, and houses.

Devil's Hopyard—Hamburg   7-1/4 mi

Description:	Quickwater, Class I-II
Date checked:	1989, SG
Navigable:	High water: February, early March
	Medium water: scratchy, late March
Scenery:	Forested, rural
Map:	USGS Hamburg
Portage:	6^1/$_4$ mi L dam at North Lyme 50 yd

Go to Devil's Hopyard State Park via Hopyard Road and put in beside the large picnic area below Chapmans Falls. Easy Class II rapids begin immediately and continue most of the way along Hopyard Road to CT 82. A couple of pitches, including a washed-out dam at the beginning of an East Haddam land-trust nature preserve, can be lined if too tricky, but most should be runnable by canoeists attempting this river at suitable flows. A low bridge at Dolbia Hill Road may have to be portaged at high water levels; watch for old wire fences along the fields below. Fallen trees will be a hazard throughout most of the run.

Below the CT 82 bridge (3 mi) the river is mostly quickwater with some easy Class II drops. Beside a cabin there is a small dam that can be easily lined on the right. The river flows under the CT 156 bridge (3^3/$_4$ mi) and is immediately joined by the East Branch (also runnable in highwater, but more challenging).

Small dams described in previous editions are now gone or obscured by the highwater necessary to make this run. The quickwater below CT 156 gives way to an old millpond owned by the Lyme land trust. The 10-foot dam (a mom and pop hydro company) is at $6^1/4$ miles and the steep portage is to the left. The remaining mile is quickwater that gives way to tidewater at the Joshuatown bridge, which is a convenient take-out spot (upstream side, left). The remaining 2 miles of the river (Hamburg Cove) is tidal, ringed with yacht moorings and expensive homes, and scenic, but there are no good take-out spots. Paddlers wishing to go to the mouth are advised to enter the Connecticut River and paddle about 2 miles downstream to the village of Essex and take out at the foot of Main Street.

Chapter 5

Thames Watershed

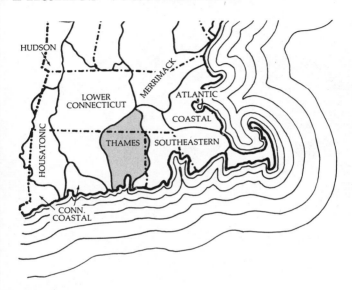

THAMES WATERSHED

Sturbridge
Oxford
Webster
Quinebaug River
French River
MA
CT
Stafford Springs
Phoenixville
Five Mile River
Willimantic River
Warrenville
Mount Hope River
Natchaug River
Danielson
Eagleville
Almyville
Andover
Hop River
North Windham
Moosup River
Willimantic
Shetucket River
Quinebaug River
Susquetonscut Brook
Baltic
Jewett City
Yantic River
Yantic
Fitchville
Norwich
Thames River
N
New London

Scale in miles

| 0 | 5 | 10 | 15 | 20 | 25 | 30 |

The rivers of the Thames Watershed are less well-known than the others in the Guide. Apparently this area is overlooked because better alternatives lie nearby or equally suitable rivers are closer to population centers. Whitewater in the Thames Watershed does not equal that found on the Quaboag and Salmon rivers to the north and west, and to the east there are many fine flatwater rivers. But, for spring and fall canoeing, these rivers offer several good trips. If you want a gentle stream with a good current, try the Willimantic. The Hop River is more difficult—narrower and faster with sharper turns. And the Natchaug River has many scenic miles of intermittent quickwater and Class I-II rapids.

The Thames River is a wide, tidal river that flows south from Norwich to Long Island Sound at New London. It is not described in this book.

YANTIC RIVER   CT

The Yantic flows eastward and joins the Thames River in Norwich. In the early spring it has some excellent whitewater, but to run all of it you must portage around two dams. The portages are not difficult. It takes two to three hours to run the section described here.

The Yantic River is smaller than the Salmon River (nearby in the Lower Connecticut Watershed) and the rapids are somewhat harder. In general, the scenery is not as nice, but some sections are attractive.

Camp Moween Road—Fitchville   5¼ mi

Description:	Lake, flatwater, quickwater, **Class I-II**
Date checked:	1985
Navigable:	High and medium water: March
Scenery:	Forested, rural, towns
Map:	USGS Fitchville
Portage:	2 mi L dam 150 yd
	2½ mi e dam at Gilman 70-300 yd

From exit 22 off CT 2, follow the road upstream along the north side of the Yantic River for 1 1/3 miles to Camp Moween Road on the left.

At the beginning the current is fast, and there are a few trees down over the river. After a mile, however, rapids begin, and there is a sharp Class II drop as the river passes alongside CT 2. Soon you reach the short deadwater behind the first dam (2 mi). Take out on the left bank just before a large boulder, carry across the road, and put in below the second bridge. Class II rapids continue for 1/4 mile to the next bridge, where the deadwater behind the dam at Gilman begins. Portage the latter on the left.

Just below this second dam (2 1/2 mi) it will probably be necessary to line down a ledge beside a factory. If the river is too high, there may be no place to stand beside the river, making it necessary to portage on the right from the dam to the bridge below it, about 300 yards.

Below Gilman (2 3/4 mi) there are easier Class II rapids that continue for 1/2 mile to a power line crossing. The remaining 1 3/4 miles to Fitchville Pond are mostly quickwater with a few Class I rapids that begin beside a cemetery and continue a short way past a road bridge below. Take out at the road leading to exit 23 off CT 2 (5 1/4 mi).

Fitchville—Norwich   3 mi

The river below here is not as attractive. Portage the dam on Fitchville Pond by going through a backyard on the left. Now along the river are several old dumps and many wrecked cars lining fields. Although there are no rapids to speak of, there is quickwater for 2 miles to the abandoned highway bridge just below the CT 32 bridge in Yantic. Beyond, the river soon flows into Norwich, where there is even less to recommend it.

SHETUCKET RIVER   CT

This river begins at the confluence of the Natchaug and Willimantic rivers and flows into the Quinebaug near Norwich. It makes a pleasant, easy run with no rapids. The wooded banks over much of the way make this an attractive trip, although there is no outstanding scenery.

Willimantic—Baltic   **12 mi**

Description:	Flatwater, quickwater
Date checked:	1989, SS
Navigable:	Passable at most water levels
Scenery:	Forested, settled
Maps:	USGS Willimantic, Scotland, Baltic
Portage:	8 mi R dam
	(12 mi R dam)

Begin on the Natchaug River at Lauter Park off CT 195 in Willimantic. The Shetucket starts at the confluence of the Willimantic in 1¹/₂ miles. The CT 203 bridge in South Windham offers a possible take-out at 4³/₄ miles. Portage the Scotland Dam on the right (8 mi). **Caution!** Stay away from the dam.

The water level below the dam is controlled by the dam. Expect a scratchy trip to Baltic with some canoe dragging if the dam is closed. It is possible to take out 100 yards below the dam on the left by carrying across the railroad track to Jerusalem Road. There are two take-outs in Baltic—just above the CT 97 bridge on the left, or at the baseball field on the right.

Baltic—Quinebaug River   **5¹/₄ mi**

This section is not recommended due to the frequent portages. In addition to the dam at Baltic, which should be portaged on the right, there are two more dams: the one at Occum (2¹/₄ mi) and the one at Taftville (4¹/₂ mi). Take out at CT 12 just above the confluence (5¹/₄ mi).

WILLIMANTIC RIVER   **CT**

The Willimantic River begins at Stafford Springs and flows south to join the Natchaug River in the city of Willimantic to form the Shetucket River.

This stream has a good current with alternate riffles and quickwater. It provides a good introduction for canoeists wishing to try river paddling for the first time. There are no tricky drops, and a road is always nearby.

The scenery is attractive for most of the way, but there are occasional sand and gravel operations and at least one modern sewage treatment plant, although it is not obtrusive. The stream is stocked with trout by the state and the water is relatively clean.

Stafford Springs—Eagleville   14³/₄ mi

Description:	Lake, **flatwater, quickwater**
Date checked:	1985
Navigable:	High or medium water: spring and fall
Scenery:	Forested, towns, settled
Maps:	USGS Stafford Springs, South Coventry

Put in just below the center of Stafford Springs where CT 32 comes close to the river. After a short distance there is a broken dam with large, concrete abutments on each side. It can be run on the left. The river then runs for several miles in a narrow valley that widens somewhat as you approach the I-86/CT 15 bridge (4³/₄ mi). The current remains steady for the length of the trip. In West Willington, US 44 (6 mi) crosses the river, as do several other roads before Mansfield Depot (12¹/₂ mi), where US 44A crosses. After another 1¹/₂ miles you reach Eagleville Lake. Take out next to the dam (14³/₄ mi), where there is a large parking area.

Eagleville—Willimantic   9 mi

Maps:	USGS Columbia, Willimantic

Below the Eagleville dam, the current lessens. The river winds past the mouth of the Hop River (5³/₄ mi), which enters on the right just below I-84, to reach a good take-out on the right at a roadside picnic area off US 6 (6 mi). Farther downstream in Willimantic there are dams and difficult rapids.

HOP RIVER CT

This clear, narrow river with abundant wildlife flows east to the Willimantic River. US 6 follows it closely but is not generally noticeable. Avoid the first three weeks of fishing season.

Andover—Willimantic 12 mi

Description:	**Flatwater, quickwater,** Class I
Date checked:	1989, EB
Navigable:	High or medium water: early spring, late fall
Scenery:	Forested, rural
Maps:	USGS Rockville, Marlborough, Columbia, Willimantic
Portage:	7 mi L dam at Hop River Rd. 10 yd

Put in on Hendee Road off US 6 in Andover, near a restaurant, 2 miles east of Bolton Notch. There is a short Class I rapid (1 mile) below a broken dam. There are slight drops at each bridge. The dam at the Hop River Road bridge (7 mi) must be portaged on the left. This is a possible take-out. After the dam, pass under another bridge, then US 6, then a power line. The next railroad bridge (10¼ mi) has a sharp Class II drop, passable only on the extreme left. It can be portaged with difficulty on the right. The next bridge is Flanders bridge, with a possible take-out (10½ mi). The next take-out is on the right on the Willimantic River just before the CT 66 bridge.

NATCHAUG RIVER CT

This is a very scenic river that flows south through a lightly settled valley to Willimantic. The lower section has been ponded by a flood control dam and reservoir. What remains provides a wide variety of rapids, ranging from rapids suitable for novices above the England Road bridge to an excellent series of Class II rapids below the CT 198 bridge, and to the exciting Class IV Diana's Pool section.

A heavy rain often provides suitable water for paddling, especially in the Diana's Pool section. The upper portion of the river is bordered by Natchaug State Forest.

Phoenixville—England Road   7¹/₄ mi

Description:	**Quickwater,** Class I-II
Date checked:	1989, SS
Navigable:	High and medium water: early spring, late fall
Maps:	USGS Hampton, Spring Hill

Put in below the junction of CT 198 and US 44 at the bridge just off General Lyons Road to avoid a dam. At the start there are 200 yards of Class II rapids, which ease up to a 2 mile mix of flatwater, quickwater, and Class I water. An alternate put-in is at a state picnic area on the right, just above ³/₄ mile of Class I and II rapids. Past a private campground there are two rock dams that may require carrying; a third dam (4¹/₂ mi) is ¹/₂ mile below the second bridge, which is Morey Road. Just past this dam there are intermittent Class II rapids that continue past the third bridge (4³/₄ mi) and ease up as you approach the crossing of Bear Hill Road (6¹/₄ mi). The next mile to the England Road bridge is flat.

England Road—North Windham   5¹/₂ mi

Description:	Flatwater, quickwater, Class II, IV
Date checked:	1989, SS
Navigable:	High and medium water: early spring, late fall, after heavy rain
Scenery:	Forested
Maps:	USGS Hampton, Spring Hill

Just at the England Road bridge there is a short drop, followed by intermittent Class II rapids that lead to a large pool. **Caution!** After the short rapids leading out of the pool, stop on the left bank to scout Mousetrap, the first Diana's Pool rapid. A large boulder forms an island, with the exciting route on the right and the sneak route on the left. Stop on the left below the outrun rapid to scout the big drop—Cow Sluice—that drops into a beautiful pool. The ledgy rapid following the pool has an undercut rock on the left, so go right.

An alternate put-in for those not wishing to run Class IV rapids is found at the CT 198 bridge. A 3/4 mile section of Class II rapids leads to 2 miles of quickwater to North Windham. The most convenient take-out is above the bridge in North Windham (3³/4 mi), on the left.

After another ¹/2 mile of mixed quickwater and Class I rapids, the Natchaug flows into the backwater behind the Mansfield Hollow Flood Control Dam. You can take out at Mansfield Hollow State Park (4 mi), but you should spot the take-out in advance so that you will recognize it from the river. The only good take-out from the lake is at the landing on Bassett Bridge Road (5¹/2 mi), which can be reached by continuing straight along the road that crosses the river at North Windham.

There is a wooden gauge on the right bank above the CT 198 bridge. 1.25 is considered minimum with 4.0 (top of gauge) considered high.

MOUNT HOPE RIVER   CT

This river is a tributary of the Natchaug River a short distance north of Willimantic. It is a small, clear stream in a predominantly rural setting. Its level of difficulty resembles the Natchaug, but relatively higher water is needed for good passage.

There are some nice Class II rapids in the last 1³/4 miles of the river, but the only convenient take-out at the end is from the Mansfield Hollow Reservoir, which may still be frozen early in the season.

Warrenville—Mansfield Hollow Reservoir   8 mi

Description:	Lake, **flatwater, quickwater,** Class I-II
Date checked:	1985
Navigable:	High water: March
Scenery:	Forested, rural, settled
Map:	USGS Spring Hill

Begin at the CT 89 bridge north of US 44 at Warrenville. Above that point access to the river is restricted, and passage down it is obstructed by fences.

A mixture of flatwater and quickwater extends for $3^1/4$ miles past the US 44 bridge ($^1/2$ mi) and the next CT 89 bridge ($2^1/4$ mi). Then there is a narrow, 100-yard Class II rapid that extends around a left turn. Easier, intermittent rapids are found in the next $^1/4$ mile to Mount Hope Bridge ($3^1/2$ mi), which is next to a traffic light.

For $2^1/4$ miles flatwater and quickwater continue almost all the way to the second small bridge below Mount Hope Bridge. Then there are nearly continuous Class I and II rapids for 1 mile to Atwoodville, where there is a sharp right turn from which a high bridge is visible. Below this turn, but above the bridge, there is a sharp drop over a ledge, which can be lined or portaged on the left. Access to the river near this bridge is poor.

More Class II rapids after the ledge in Atwoodville ($6^3/4$ mi) culminate in a short, steep Class II-III pitch just above the normal pool ($7^1/2$ mi) behind the Mansfield Hollow Flood Control Dam. The most convenient take-out is at the bridge on Bassett Bridge Road off CT 195 in Mansfield Center, on the Natchaug River.

QUINEBAUG RIVER   MA, CT

Maps:	USGS Wales, Southbridge, Webster, Putnam, Danielson, Plainfield, Jewett City, Norwich

The Quinebaug River rises in Holland on the Massachusetts-Connecticut line, flows in a big loop to the north and east through Brimfield, Sturbridge, and Southbridge, and crosses the state line flowing southeast at Dudley. It then flows south through Putnam, Danielson, and Jewett City until it turns west to join the Shetucket River near Taftville and the Thames River at Norwich. There are a number of dams, some of which are no problem and others, particularly in urban areas, that must be approached with considerable caution. The water is dark and in places somewhat polluted, but there is much pleasant canoeing available on this stream.

Hamilton Reservoir—East Brimfield   **5 mi**

If water is high enough, the 1 1/2 mile stream below Hamilton
Reservoir is a pretty run, but be prepared to lift across a few shallow,
rocky places and ledges. If water is low (one judges by the flow over
the dam) a portage can be made by foot or by auto about 1 mile via
Dug Hill Road to Holland Pond Recreation Area (USCE), which is a
good put-in at any water stage. From the outlet of Holland Pond, the
river flows as a broad, placid stream. In 1/2 mile there is a road bridge
and a camping spot on the left. Mill Brook enters from the left here
and can be used as an alternate starting point from Brimfield. The
Quinebaug continues as a broad stream for 3 miles through open
marshes bordered by pretty hills, and soon widens into the
permanent pool behind East Brimfield is a flood control dam. An
extension of the lake stretches north of US 20, forming what was
previously Long Pond. There is a good take-out place at its north tip.

East Brimfield Dam—Sturbridge   **2 3/4 mi**

Below the East Brimfield flood control dam there is 3/4 mile of
riffles, easily run if the release from the dam is around 120 cfs (2.7
feet on the tailrace marker). A broken dam just around the bend
below Holland Road bridge should be scouted before running. The
dams in Fiskdale can be portaged on the left and over the dam. The
river is then fast flowing for 1 mile to Leadmine Road bridge and the
pond at Old Sturbridge Village.

Sturbridge—Westville Dam   **5 3/4 mi**

At Old Sturbridge Village, there is a dam that is portaged easily
on the left. For the next 4 miles the Quinebaug is a pretty, placid
stream with few rapids, running through woods and marshy
meadows. There is then a low dam to portage, left, or to take out
onto autos, right. The river descends 20 feet in the next 3/4 mile to the
head of the permanent lake, 1 mile long, at Westville Flood Control
Dam. This twenty-foot descent has both heavy and thin spots, with
much depending on the amount of water being released from the
East Brimfield dam. Scout this section before running it.

Westville Dam—West Dudley   5^1/$_2$ mi

This section is not pleasant. It is best to take out either at the head of the lake at the Westville dam, where there is a boat ramp and parking area on the left, or at the low dam ^{3}/$_4$ mile upriver, and then to portage by auto around the entire city of Southbridge. For those who are willing to labor up and over the Westville dam, there is ^{1}/$_2$ mile of rapids, easy if the water release is adequate, to a small millpond below the Mill Street bridge in Southbridge, where there is another dam to portage. Then another ^{1}/$_2$ mile of easy rapids leads to the millpond at American Optical Company. Canoes must be taken out at the Mechanic Street Bridge at the head of this pond and portaged 1 mile via Mechanic Street and MA 131. This bypasses one dam on the American Optical grounds and another about ^{1}/$_2$ mile below. Return canoes to the river below the second dam. It is then 2^1/$_2$ miles, mostly slackwater and foul, to the dam at West Dudley.

West Dudley—West Thompson   10 mi

Below Southbridge the river runs through a broad valley with bushes on the banks and cultivated fields or meadows on the flood plain. The bridge at Dudley Hill Road is a possible put-in, if one has portaged around Southbridge by auto. Or drive 2 miles farther and put in below the dam at West Dudley, avoiding some of the foul water below Southbridge. From West Dudley the river runs with fair current to the broken dam at Fabyan, which can be run through the open sluice. It is then 6 miles to the flood-control dam at West Thompson. The French River enters just below this dam.

West Thompson—Jewett City   33 mi

One can put in below the dam at West Thompson and run 2 miles to Putnam, but as there are three dams in quick succession there, many will prefer to put in below Putnam. Be cautious approaching the upper dam at Putnam, and make a landing on the left, well upstream from the dam. A single carry of ^{3}/$_4$ mile via city streets bypasses all three dams. From the third dam the river meanders somewhat for the next 12 miles to Danielson, flowing through broad flood plains for much of the distance. The only interruptions come about midway, where there are two road bridges 1/2 mile apart, the second being CT 101; 1/2 mile farther is a dam that can be portaged easily on either side. Care must be taken at Danielson. The first dam can be portaged on the left, starting on the downriver side of the new US 6 bridge, but be cautious about currents. The Five Mile River enters here from the left through culverts under the new rotary. The next 1/4 mile involves broken dams and heavy rapids that should not be attempted without a careful scouting of their entire length. Portage around them on the left if not thoroughly expert in such water. Below Danielson 1 1/2 miles are the broken remains of Dyer Dam, which should be scouted from the right bank. Another 2 1/2 miles brings one to Wauregan, where the jagged remains of a broken dam must be avoided. It is best portaged left, near the sluice gates to avoid the fast current sweeping into the jaws of the break.

The section from Wauregan to Jewett City offers pleasant canoeing. It is 6 miles without interruption through well-wooded country to the CT 14 bridge near Canterbury, with the Moosup River entering from the left early in this stretch. From CT 14, the river meanders 5 miles through broad flood plain to the next road bridge and railroad crossing near the head of Aspinook Pond. Another 3 miles of lake paddling brings one to the dam at Jewett City, where the drop is vertical for twenty feet. Portage here is on the right, starting well upstream from the strong current at the masonry wing wall at the approach to the crest of the dam.

Jewett City—Norwich   11 mi

The river now flows through a narrow valley between steep, wooded hills. It is a picturesque stretch but not an area for novices, as there are problem rocks and currents; it is very difficult to take out along the way. About 3 miles below Jewett City, the river makes a sharp right to flow west for 1 mile, then south 1 mile, and then west again for 1 mile, entering a narrow gorge at the far end of which is the tall and dangerous power dam at Connecticut Light and Power Company's Tunnel Plant. This gorge and dam can be a trap if the water is high enough to flow over the crest of the dam. Water levels are subject to unexpected change as they depend partly on operations at the power plant. There are no stillwaters in which to take refuge. The current will sweep full force through the gorge and over the dam. Do not venture into this gorge without having first walked to the dam, accessible by a dirt road and footbridge from CT 12, to assess the situation on the day of the trip, and having inquired about aniticipated water levels at the hour of the expected arrival. If water is being taken through the plant to the extent that there is little or no flow over the crest of the dam at arrival time, a landing can be made against the rock cliff at the right end of the crest, followed by a difficult and very hazardous portage 200 yards along the middle of the railroad track to the far end of its masonry retaining wall, which drops off vertically twenty feet into the river bed. Then scramble down the steep rock-fill to the water's edge, and load and launch from the rocks in deep water. The railroad track is in active use, and it has blind curves at both approaches to the portage area. The best advice is to stay away from this area entirely. One-quarter mile below the power dam, the Shetucket River enters from the right. One mile farther is the dam at Norwich, which is best portaged on the left. Another $1^1/2$ miles through Norwich brings one to the junction with the Yantic River on the right, forming the Thames River.

FRENCH RIVER   MA

Maps:	USGS Leicester, Webster, Oxford

The French River rises in a cluster of ponds on the border between Leicester and Spencer, where the canoeist can find some pleasant lake-paddling. From there it flows south through a rapid succession of shallow brooks, millponds, and dams to Hodges Village Flood Control Dam in Oxford. The run from there to Webster is quite pretty and without dams. Below Webster the dams are frequent and the water vile until the river joins the Quinebaug just below West Thompson dam.

Oxford—Webster 8 mi

When there is a good flow of water, a start can be made from the area in North Oxford west of CT 12 opposite Old Worcester Road, about 2³/₄ miles above Hodges Village Flood Control Dam. Another good starting point is in the pond just below the dam. The river is placid and pretty for the next 5¹/₂ miles to the dam at North Village in Webster. Mill Brook, the outlet of Webster Lake, enters from the left 200 yards upstream from the high abandoned railroad bridge at North Village. At this point, the water becomes opaque and malodorous. A take-out at this point is recommended.

FIVE MILE RIVER CT

Maps: USGS Thompson, East Killingly, Danielson

The Five Mile River rises in Thompson near the south end of Webster Lake. It flows south into Quaddick Reservoir, continues south through Putnam into Killingly, and then swings southwest and then south again to meet the Quinebaug River at Danielson. Much of it flows through wild, unspoiled country, mostly woods, but some of it through open farmland. It appears to hold its water well, and parts of it can probably be run even in the summer.

Quaddick Reservoir—Ballouville 8 mi

There are several possible routes from the outlet of the Quaddick Reservoir. Carry over the dam into the small pond, and then carry over the pond's dam and through the brush into the stream below. Or bypass the small pond and second dam by carrying 400 yards along the road on the right. From the road bridge just below the second dam there are 200 yards of brook to the next pond, and this may be a scratchy stretch if the water is low. The portage can be continued through an open field to the second pond, if necessary. The next 5 miles of stream will have some shallow, scratchy spots if the water is not well up until reaching the slackwater at the bridge 1 mile above Pineville Dam. The run is narrow and winding, through farmland and well-wooded areas. At Pineville there is a fine swimming hole above the stone dam, and an easy portage, left. If the water is too low to navigate the riffles below the dam, carry 700 yards along the paved road to the next bridge, where the slackwater above Ballouville Dam begins.

Ballouville—Danielson   7 mi

At Ballouville, land between the dam spillway and the gatehouse on the left. If the water is too low to run the riffles below the dam, portage 600 yards left around the mill via streets and put in at the canal below the mill. About 1 mile beyond Ballouville is a drop that should be looked at before running. There are a number of little drops over ledges throughout this $1^1/2$-mile run to Attawaugan, which can be impassable during low water. There is a low dam to be portaged just above CT 12, and a good flow of water is needed to navigate the next mile to the slackwater above Killingly. There are probably two short portages around obstructions in this stretch. At Killingly, carry 600 yards via streets, starting from the first spillway and sluice gates and going around the right side of the factory. Or portage 300 yards along the embankment left of the millpool to the second spillway, scrambling down through the poison ivy to enter the river at the foot of the spillway. The river below is shallow and scratchy during low water until slackwater is reached above the Rock Avenue bridge $1^1/2$ miles below Killingly. Another $2^1/2$ miles of slackwater leads to the center of Danielson, where there is a dam.

MOOSUP RIVER   RI, CT

Maps: USGS Oneco, Plainfield

The Moosup River rises in Rhode Island, flowing south at first, then swinging westward through the towns of Moosup and Central Village to join the Quinebaug below Wauregan. Its upper portion offers remote, wilderness canoeing. Above Almyville, however, there are many fallen trees, and it should only be run in the spring. Its central part has frequent dams, and its final stretch is wooded and remote.

Moosup Valley—Quinebaug River   **23 mi**

Start at the CT 14 bridge near Fairbanks Corner. From there the river runs a good 6 miles to Oneco, meandering through isolated, wild, wooded country most of the way. The dam at Oneco is portaged by starting at the landing on the left side above the highway bridge, crossing the bridge, and putting in behind the mill on the right. It is then 2 miles with riffles to the dam at Sterling, where the portage is on the far right near the mill and runs 100 yards along CT 14 to the Main Street bridge. In another 3 miles the high upper dam at Almyville is reached. Here the portage can be made on either side, carrying around the mill buildings. The topographic map (1953) shows five dams in the next 3½ miles, but two of these have since broken, making a reasonably fast river with some boulder-dodging. The dam below Almyville is easily portaged on the right if one is not concerned about poison ivy. The river runs fast for the next mile to the broken upper dam at Moosup, which experienced whitewater canoeists will likely find runnable, and others can easily lift over on the left. The second dam at Moosup is broken, and it has been replaced by a low dam, easily portaged, located at the head of the old pond. The river continues through the dry bed of the old pond to a 1-foot drop located at the site of the old dam. This and the short rubble pile below are easily portaged. Just beyond the Connecticut Turnpike (I-95) there is a brief portage over the left end of a low dam. The map does not show the next low dam just ahead, located 150 yards above the CT 12 bridge. At Central Village there is a 1-foot drop at the railroad bridge to run or lift over. Fifty yards ahead are the remains of the old dam shown on the map, which can be run. One-half mile farther are two road bridges, which are the last take-out points on the Moosup River. The next take-out beyond these bridges is at CT 14, 6 miles downstream: two miles of the Moosup River to its junction with the Quinebaug, then 4 miles on the Quinebaug.

Chapter 6

Southeastern Watersheds

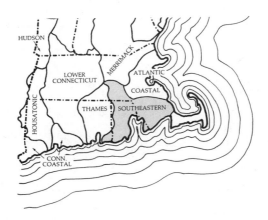

SOUTHEASTERN WATERSHEDS

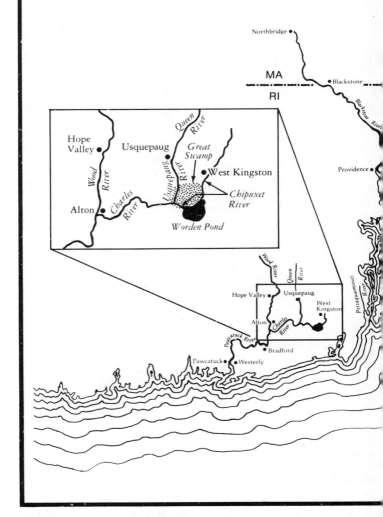

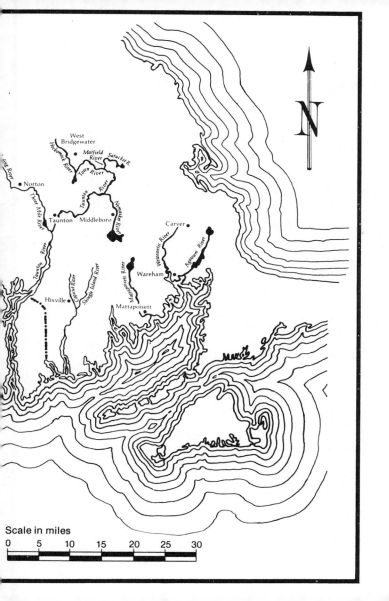

Scale in miles

0 5 10 15 20 25 30

The rivers of the Southeastern Watersheds surprisingly have remained undeveloped despite their proximity to large urban areas. They offer many miles of canoeing amid surroundings that are relatively unspoiled.

The Blackstone, Chipuxet, Matfield, Nemasket, Satucket, Taunton, and Town rivers can be canoed whenever they are not frozen. Parts of the Agawam, North, Pawcatuck, and Wood rivers are also runnable throughout the canoeing season.

The cleanest and clearest river is the Agawam, followed at some distance by the Nemasket. The award for the darkest, clean river (or the cleanest, dark river) goes to the Mattapoisett. The Taunton wins, uncontested, the prize for most polluted, although it is not too noticeable at high water.

WAMPANOAG COMMEMORATIVE   MA
CANOE PASSAGE

The Wampanoag Commemorative Canoe Passage follows inland waterways that were used by the Wampanoag Indians, who lived in southeastern Massachusetts. It connects the Massachusetts and Narragansett bays.

From Massachusetts Bay, it follows the North River past Hanover and heads south along Herring Brook to Furnace Pond in Pembroke. Then it crosses over to the Taunton River watershed via Little Sandy Pond. It goes through Stetson Pond, the twin Monponsett Ponds, and ultimately reaches Robbins Pond in East Bridgewater via Stump Brook. From Robbins Pond it follows the Satucket, Matfield, and Taunton rivers.

In chapter 7 there are descriptions of those portions of the Canoe Passage that follow the North River at the Massachusetts Bay end, and in this chapter the Satucket, Matfield, and Taunton rivers from Robbins Pond to the city of Taunton: a total of almost 41 miles. The connecting link of about 12 miles is described in *Wampanoag Commemorative Canoe Passage*, a booklet available free from the Plymouth County Development Council, Box 1620, Pembroke, MA 02359.

PAWCATUCK RIVER   RI, CT

The Pawcatuck River drains much of southern Rhode Island. It rises under the name of the Queens River in West Greenwich and flows south to Usquepaug Village in South Kingstown. It is known as the Usquepaug River from here through the Great Swamp to the outlet from Worden Pond; then it is called the Charles River until it meets the Wood River south of Alton. From there it is the Pawcatuck as it flows south to the sea at Watch Hill, Rhode Island.

This is a very pleasant and interesting trip through three Rhode Island management areas, where there is good warm-water fishing. There are campsites along the river in the Carolina and Burlingame management areas. It is 29^1/$_2$ miles from Usquepaug to Westerly.

Wood River—Westerly   15^1/$_4$ mi

Description:	**Flatwater,** Class I-II
Date checked:	1985
Navigable:	Passable at all water levels
Scenery:	Forested, rural, towns
Maps:	USGS Carolina, Ashaway
Portages:	4^3/$_4$ mi R Bradford Dam 20 yd
	11^1/$_4$ mi R Potter Hill Dam 100 yd
Campsites:	2^1/$_4$ mi L Burlingame Management Area—state
	2^3/$_4$ mi L Indian Acres Canoe Camp

With occasional, broad meanders, the Pawcatuck River winds past open fields and swamps from the confluence of the Charles and Wood rivers to Westerly. There is an abandoned milltown at Burdickville near the beginning, but most of the river is remote with relatively few houses.

Below the confluence of the Charles and Wood rivers, forming the Pawcatuck, it is a mile to the broken dam at Burdickville. Run it on the right or carry 30 yards on the left. Then the river is wide and flat. At the Burlingame Management Area, where the river runs due south, there is a campsite on the left bank. Then in about ^{1}/$_2$ mile, where the river runs due north, you reach Indian Acres Canoe

Campsite. The river meanders for 2 miles to Bradford, where there is a Fisherman's Access at the RI 91/216 bridge (4³/4 mi). About 50 yards past the bridge, portage 20 yards on the right around a broken 4-foot mill-dam. Then there are 6¹/2 miles of flatwater past the RI 3 bridge (10 mi) to the dam at Potter Hill (ll¹/4 mi). Take out on the right just before the bridge. Carry 100 yards down Laurel Street, past the fish ladder at the 8-foot dam.

Below the Potter Hill bridge (ll¹/4 mi) there is a short stretch of rapids, then flatwater to Boom Bridge (13¹/4 mi). From there it is 1¹/4 miles to White Rock.

Caution! At White Rock there is an old debris-covered dam that shunts most of the river into a canal on the left. The current then becomes strong with some occasional rocks. The rapids are an easy Class II, but there are few places to land once you are in the canal. Keep to the right. After 500 yards the river flows through a breach in the canal wall and returns to the old streambed. At the quick s turn there are some Class II rapids, which present no problem to capable canoeists as long as the channel is not blocked by debris. If you wish to scout this area, stop on the left above the old dam.

The best take-out is just before the new RI 78 bridge (15¹/4 mi), which can be reached from White Rock Road on the east bank.

Below Westerly   **3 mi**

The river flows between the towns of Pawcatuck and Westerly. **Caution!** Just below the Stillman Avenue bridge is an old breached dam that can be run on the left at certain water levels, when it may be Class II with large waves. Scout this in advance.

Just before the river empties into Little Narragansett Bay there will be one more dam to portage. This spot is marked by the evidence of a boat yard. An old wooden building will appear to block the river and the right bank will have wooden retaining walls. Portage on the right.

After this portage the river merges with saltwater, and there is the danger of large, fast powerboats. You may continue another 2 miles and take out at some of the boat yards or yacht clubs on the left bank. Be sure to ask permission in advance to leave a car there.

WOOD RIVER   **RI**

The Wood River rises in western Rhode Island and flows south to Alton, where it joins the Pawcatuck. It is one of the most attractive streams in the area. It flows through the Arcadia Management Area. The most popular section of the river starts at the RI 165 bridge and runs for 13¹/₄ miles to Alton. This section is always passable.

West Greenwich—Pawcatuck River   16¹/₂ mi

Description:	Lakes, **flatwater,** quickwater, Class I
Date checked:	1989, GE
Navigable:	Above RI 165, high or medium water: January through May
	Passable at all water levels below RI 165
Scenery:	Forested, rural, towns
Maps:	USGS Hope Valley, Carolina
Portages:	6 mi L Barberville Dam 70 yd
	8¹/₂ mi L Wyoming Dam 200 yd
	9¹/₂ mi R Hope Valley Dam 100 yd
	13¹/₄ mi e Woodville Dam 70 yd
	15³/₄ mi R Alton Dam 100 yd

From RI 3, head west on RI 165 for 5¹/₄ miles to Escoheag Hill Road. Go north for about 1 mile to the first right. Take the dirt road down a steep hill to the river.

For the first 2¹/₂ miles to RI 165, the river is narrow and shallow. Most of the way there is quickwater with sharp turns.

A parking area on river left, 50 yards downstream of the RI 165 bridge (2¹/₂ mi), provides good access. Two miles of quickwater are followed by 1¹/₂ miles of deadwater to the Barberville Dam. The rapids below the dam are shallow in low water and should be carried while carrying the dam.

Below Barberville Dam (6 mi) there is good current, then a mile of flatwater to Wyoming Pond at Skunk Hill Road. It is ³/₄ mile across the mill pond to the dam at the junction of RI 3 and RI 138, a favorite swimming spot.

The river is shallow below the Wyoming Dam (8$^1/_2$ mi), and it is suggested that you portage 300 yards down RI 3 to the next bridge and put in below a power station. In another mile, portage the Hope Valley Dam. Take out on the right, cross the road, and put in 25 yards downstream of the bridge, after passing an old mill. In 1/4 mile a 6-inch dam is easily run, and in another 1/4 mile the Wood passes under I-95. There is a state launching ramp off Hope Valley Road. It is recommended that boaters shuttle from Wyoming to this point, thereby skipping two portages.

The river then flows through woods before reaching marshland above Woodville Dam (13$^1/_4$ mi). Exotic birds are raised in this area. Portage the dam from river right and cross the bridge.

After Woodville Dam the river deepens. Turn left at a fork. Laurel is abundant in this area. Marsh and forested banks give way to 3/4 mile of ponding above Aldon Dam (15$^3/_4$ mi), where there is a state launching area on the right.

At Alton, a portage of 100 yards on the right is followed by $^3/_4$ mile of flatwater to the confluence with the Pawcatuck River (16$^1/_2$ mi).

CHARLES RIVER   RI

The Charles River is formed by the confluence of the Usquepaug River and the Chipuxet River (just downstream of Worden Pond). This description starts just below there and ends at the confluence of the Charles and Wood rivers, which is the beginning of the Pawcatuck River.

The old mill towns along the way are much the same as they were in the 1700's. From the parking lot at the Kenyon Mill, walk up the hill and visit the mill store. In Shannock, the house on the high dam was built in 1709.

A suggested 2-or 3-day trip of about 18 miles starts at the Worden Pond Fishermen's Access on the southern shore and ends at the Bradford Fishermen's Access of RI 91/216 on the Pawcatuck River.

Biscuit City Landing—Wood River   8³/₄ mi

Description:	**Flatwater,** Class II
Date checked:	1985
Navigable:	High and medium water: January through June, after heavy rain
Scenery:	Forested, towns
Maps:	USGS Kingston, Carolina
Portages:	³/₄ mi L dam in Kenyon 20 yd
	1¹/₂ mi L high dam in Shannock 20 yd
	1³/₄ mi R low dam in Shannock 100 yd
	3¹/₂ mi L dam in Carolina 70 yd
Campsite:	4 mi L Carolina Management area—state

To reach the Fishermen's Access off RI 2, take Biscuit City Road about ¹/₂ mile north of the railroad crossing in Kenyon.

There is flatwater past the high, arched, concrete RI 2 bridge (¹/₂ mi) to the dam at Kenyon (³/₄ mi). Portage on the left 50 feet. There is less than a mile of flatwater to the high dam at Shannock. The carry is on the left for 50 feet; put in under the bridge. A short distance beyond is the low dam, which has been run, but this is not advised. The carry here is on the right. This dam is built at old Indian fishing falls and a fight over usage once occurred here between the Pequot and Narrangansett Indian tribes. A plaque is on the right bank. Then there is flatwater to Carolina (3¹/₂ mi), where there is a dam at RI 112, which crosses the river on three bridges.

Below the left-hand bridge at Carolina, there is a Class II chute in high water that should be scouted. It is followed by 1/4 mile of easy Class II rapids that are very scratchy in low water. At Richmond (5¹/₄ mi) there is a Fisherman's Access off RI 91 next to a dam that is runnable in the center.

Below the Richmond dam (5¹/₄ mi) there is a good current for 1¹/₄ miles to a wooden bridge (6¹/₂ mi). In the last 2¹/₄ miles to the confluence with the Wood River (8³/₄ mi), there are about half a dozen large trees across the river.

CHIPUXET RIVER   RI

The Chipuxet River rises in Exeter near Slocum and flows south through the Great Swamp to Worden Pond and then to the Pawcatuck River, which flows in to Little Narrangansett Bay. The entire river can be run throughout the year, but may require some dragging and skirmishes with overgrown brush.

Hundred Acre Pond—Biscuit City Landing   9³/₄ mi

Description:	Flatwater, quickwater
Date checked:	1989, PB
Navigable:	Anytime except after drought
Scenery:	Forested, wild
Maps:	USGS Slocum, Kingston

Put in at the bridge on Wolf Rocks Road just above the pond. It is about 1 mile through Hundred Acre Pond to the outlet at the south end where there are some shallow riffles under the railroad bridge. Some dragging may be necessary to Thirty Acre Pond. RI 138 crosses ¹/₂ mile below Thirty Acre Pond at Taylor's Access (2 mi), an alternate put-in. The Chipuxet then flows through the Great Swamp, one of Rhode Island's natural treasures. To shuttle, go west on RI 138, south on RI 2, and left on Biscuit City Road.

One-half mile below Taylor's Access a railroad bridge is passed, with Worden Pond 2 miles farther. Caution should be exercised on Worden Pond, as it is shallow and gets choppy in a southerly wind. It is possible to paddle left to cottages that line the east shore in bad weather. In good weather, keep the island to your left as you paddls southwest 1 mile to Stony Point. The route goes around Stony Point and southwest to the next point. An old seaplane hanger can be seen in the cove to your right. Follow the south shore of the point until you reach the outlet, where you will re-enter the swamp (6³/₄ mi).

Here the river is narrow, winding, and enclosed by brush. You have to barge through. In approximately 1/4 mile you will approach a dock and pump house at the Great Swamp Waterfowl Impoundment, where osprey are often sighted. Not long after the impoundment area you exit the swamp at the confluence with the Usquepaug River (10 mi). At this point the river is known as the Charles River.

In ³/₄ mile the river runs near railroad tracks. When the tracks come into view, look for a sign on the rights that says "Boat Landing." This will lead you up a small stream to the Biscuit City fisherman's access, a possible take-out. It is also possible to proceed another mile downriver, under RI 2, to the mill in Kenyon (12 mi). Take out on the right above the dam in the mill parking lot, reached by car by continuing south on RI 2 from Biscuit City and taking the first right after it crosses the river.

PETTAQUAMSCUTT RIVER   RI
(locally called NARROW RIVER)

The Pettaquamscutt River rises in North Kingston and after a short distance flows into Pausacaco Pond and thence to tidewater. The upper reaches of the river are too small for canoeing, although the pond may offer some pleasant paddling.

Gilbert Stuart Road—Mouth   6 mi

Description:	Tidal, marsh
Date checked:	1985
Navigable:	Passable at all water levels
Scenery:	Wild, forested, marsh, settled
Maps:	USGS Wickford, Narrangansett Pier

Put in from Gilbert Stuart Road. The river is about 10 feet wide and runs for about 300 feet before opening to a pond 1/4 mile in diameter. Keep left going downriver to pass through another narrow channel into a second pond, which takes on the essence of a river, with some development on the east shore; the west shore is almost entirely forested.

The river narrows slowly, and after about 2 miles reaches an underpass (Lacey Bridge), where people fish from the bridge. Development below the bridge increases. Then suddenly a fragile marsh appears on the left. Look for osprey nests 2 feet in diameter atop telephone poles. Pass under Middle Bridge, another fishing spot. Eventually the river turns left and becomes tidal.

The tide at the mouth is three feet. Tides are about the same as Newport, or about 3^{1}/2 hours earlier than Boston.

BLACKSTONE RIVER   MA

The Blackstone connects the second and third most populous cities in New England, Worcester and Providence. The Blackstone River Basin, with many small milltowns on the main river and its tributaries, is one of the most heavily industrialized in New England. A certain amount of pollution is to be expected, but the river is being cleaned up.

The Blackstone does have many scenic stretches that are away from roads and mills. The area around Rice City Pond has been set aside as a state recreation area. There are also some challenging rapids. Parts of the canal that was built to handle commerce between Worcester and Providence are still intact.

Worcester—Rockdale   11 mi

Description:	Flatwater, **quickwater,** Class **I, II,** III, IV
Date checked:	1989, RC
Navigable:	Medium to high water: April, May
Scenery:	Settled, towns, rural
Maps:	USGS Worcester South, Milford, Grafton
Portages:	^{3}/4 mi L dam
	2 mi R rapids at Millbury—optional
	2^{3}/4 mi e dam at power substation
	4 mi L dam
	5 mi e dam—optional
	6 mi L dam
	8 mi e Fisherville dam
	9 mi R Farnumsville dam

The upper Blackstone is a very enjoyable paddle in spite of its degraded (but improving) water quality and the many dams encountered. There is a good current throughout, with some whitewater. The entire Blackstone River in Massachusetts and Rhode Island is eventually to be developed as a linear park.

To reach the put-in, turn left onto Millbury Street, from MA 146, north of US 20.

Put in at the bridge 100 yards down Millbury Street near the former USS steel plant. Take the left channel at a small dam (3/4 mi) and portage. Quickwater follows below the US 20 (1 mi) and I-90 (1 1/4 mi) bridges. Mixed flatwater and quickwater continue to Millbury Center (2 mi), where a short stretch of Class II rapids will be encountered adjacent to a mill building. At 2 1/4 miles the Blackstone turns left beneath a railroad bridge and enters a 200-yard stretch of Class II-IV rapids, culminating in a narrow, rocky channel beneath the South Main Street bridge. To portage this stretch, take out to the right of the railroad bridge and follow the tracks to the road crossing. It is possible to run the Class II portion and exit on the left bank above the South Main Street bridge. This area should be scouted. Portage requires following Maple Street along the southerly bank of the river about 1/2 mile to the next bridge crossing.

A dam located at a power substation (2 3/4 mi) may be portaged on either side. At 4 miles, another portage is required at the Singing Dam. Cross the road and listen to the song. Enter the river at the base of the dam or along a dirt road and path just beyond. The breached dam in Wilkinsonville (5 mi) may be run, but a portage is suggested. The Saundersville dam (6 mi) may be directly approached on the left and walked down on the steps. The dam outlet can be entered from an eddy at the base.

At 6 1/2 miles the Blackstone divides in two. The paddler can elect to bear left where it joins with the Quinsigamond River, or turn right under the Pleasant Street bridge, which is immediately followed by a 200-yard stretch of quickwater. This is a remnant of the Blackstone Canal. A breached dam that follows can be run. At 8 miles the Blackstone enters into the pond at Fisherville, where the Quinsigamond River enters on the left. The Quinsigamond offers a pleasant 4-mile flatwater paddle from the junction of MA 122 and

MA 140 to Fisherville Pond. The Fisherville dam is breached but runnable.

At 9 miles the dam in Farnumsville is reached. Portage right. From here is it a pleasant two miles to the take-out in Rockdale (11 mi). Access to this take-out is behind the chemical company on Sutton Street in Rockdale, one block west of MA 122.

Northbridge—Blackstone   12³/₄ mi

Description:	Lake, **flatwater,** quickwater, Class I-II
Date checked:	1989, JC
Navigable:	Passable at all water levels
Scenery:	Forested, towns
Maps:	USGS Grafton, Uxbridge, Blackstone
Portages:	3 mi R dam on Rice City Pond 100 yd
	12 mi L dam above Blackstone Gorge 100 yd
	(12³/₄ mi dam)

To reach the put-in, go east of Church Street from MA 122 between Northbridge and North Uxbridge. Put in at the bridge. There are 2-1/4 miles of quickwater and many turns to Rice City Pond. At the southern end (3 mi) the river divides, and both parts spill over dams. Pass under the right-hand bridge and take out by the picnic area. This section is a portion of the Blackstone Canal. The river below the right-hand dam winds for 1³/₄ miles with quickwater around sharp corners to MA 16, just above which there is a mill on the right.

One-quarter mile below MA 16 (4³/₄ mi) the Mumford River enters on the right. The Blackstone meanders for the next 2¹/₄ miles past the mouth of the West River (6¹/₄ mi) to the MA 122 bridge (7¹/₄ mi). The river straightens somewhat for the next 3¹/₄ miles to the bridge at Millville. Here the river divides. There are Class II rapids on each side, with the left side being sportiest.

A little over 1¹/₂ miles below the Millville bridge (10¹/₂ mi), there is a large dam that is more easily portaged on the left. Below the dam the river flows through Blackstone Gorge. This is an isolated, granite gorge with 600 yards of Class III rapids that are difficult and dangerous in high water. They begin just below the dam and run through an s turn that begins to the left. They end with a turbulent chute that is best run in the middle. Scout this section from the left bank. The ownership of the gorge is in transition. You may disregard signs stating "Boats Prohibited Beyond This Point," which were erected by a previous owner.

At the end of the gorge, the Branch River (12$\frac{1}{2}$ mi) enters on the right. Shortly thereafter the outflow from the hydroelectric diversion returns to the river on the left, followed closely by the take-out, also on the left. A 5-foot dam lies under the next bridge (12$\frac{3}{4}$ mi).

The top of the gorge can be reached by travelling south on Staples Lane (a private way, shown as Rolling Dam Road on some maps) or west on County Road, both off MA 122 in Blackstone. Below the gorge the take-out is behind the old Tupperware mill at a baseball field and park. It can be reached via Old Mendon Street south of MA 122.

TAUNTON RIVER   MA

The Taunton River flows to the sea at Fall River. It is the lower segment of the largest drainage system in southeastern Massachusetts, and it forms a part of the Wampanoag Commemorative Canoe Passage.

Southwest of Brockton the Hockomock flows into the Town River, and southeast of Brockton the Satucket flows into the Matfield. In Bridgewater the Matfield and the Town rivers join to form the Taunton River. Below the city of Taunton the river is tidal, and many large cabin cruisers are berthed here.

Although there are many towns in the region through which the Taunton flows, it manages to avoid most of them. It flows along the edge of some fields, but most of the way the river is lined with thick woods and tangled underbrush. It makes a nice flatwater trip if you are willing to overlook that fact that the water is severely polluted. At low water the smell is especially noticeable.

MA 104—Taunton $21^1/_4$ mi

Description:	**Flatwater,** Class I
Date checked:	1985
Navigable:	Passable at all water levels
Scenery:	Forested, rural, towns
Maps:	USGS Bridgewater, Taunton
Portages:	0 mi R dam below MA 104 20 yd

East of Bridgewater, MA 104 crosses the Taunton River near some old factories. Just below the bridge there is a dam that backs up water on both the Matfield and Town rivers. Portage 20 yards on the right. The Winnetuxet River enters on the left after $3^1/_4$ miles.

There are many bridges across the river. The second one is partially collapsed ($3^3/_4$ mi). The fourth is a railroad bridge beside a brick factory, and then, just below a power line, is the mouth of the Nemasket River ($6^3/_4$ mi) on the left.

Under the fifth bridge, Titicut Road ($7^3/_4$ mi), are some Class I riffles. Then comes MA 18/28 ($8^1/_4$ mi). Above the next two bridges are riffles that are flooded out in high water. Then you pass under MA 25 (no access) and US 44 ($12^3/_4$ mi).

The biggest rapids, but still only Class I, are under the Church Street bridge, an old stone structure that constricts the flow of the river into several narrow passages. Many canoeists on the Taunton River lack whitewater skills, and this is where they run into trouble. The waves are biggest, and the current trickiest, in high water.

Pass below a bridge in East Taunton beside a factory at $15^1/_4$ miles and notice many long, overgrown stonewall embankments lining the riverbank as you continue downstream. After considerable winding, the river flows under MA 24 (no access). In the city of Taunton there are several more bridges beyond a closed girder bridge ($19^3/_4$ mi) next to US 44. The first bridge below the two railroad bridges is MA 140 ($21^1/_4$ mi), and the Mill River enters on the right just beyond.

At high tide there are no rapids as you pass through Taunton. High tide occurs about $2^1/_2$ hours earlier than Boston; low tide about 1 hour earlier. The tide varies between $2^1/_2$ and $3^1/_2$ feet.

HOCKOMOCK and TOWN RIVERS   **MA**

The Hockomock River flows south from Brockton to the Town River, which then flows generally eastward to Bridgewater, where it joins the Matfield River to form the Taunton River.

The Hockomock is a small, meandering stream that flows for much of its length through meadows and along the edges of fields. Most of the Hockomock Swamp is owned or controlled by the Massachusetts Division of Fisheries and Wildlife. Bushes that grow out from the banks are regularly clipped.

The Town River flows out of Nippenicket Pond in Bridgewater and, within a mile, is joined by the Hockomock. This upper section is very overgrown and passage down it is difficult. It would be a good trip if reopened. The river below the Hockomock is noticeably wider.

A good trip at high water is the 9½ miles from Walnut Street in West Bridgewater to the first dam in the same town. At low water, the 5 miles between the Scotland Street bridge in West Bridgewater and the High Street bridge in Bridgewater are recommended. The 4 miles of river below the High Street dam to MA 104 are not recommended due to pollution and debris.

West Bridgewater—High Street Dam   **12 mi**

Description:	**Flatwater,** Quickwater
Date checked:	1989, DW
Navigable:	High and medium water; March through May
	Low water, E of MA 24 only
Scenery:	Rural, settled
Maps:	USGS Brockton, Taunton, Whitman, Bridgewater
Portages:	1 mi L low bridge 10 yd
	4 mi R culvert 10 yd
	5½ mi e culvert at Maple St. 10 yd
	8 mi e Forest St. Bridge (high water only) 20 yd
	9½ mi L dam at War Memorial Park 10–100 yd

To reach the Walnut Street bridge, head west from the MA 106 exit off MA 24. Take the first right (north) and turn left at the second intersection.

Below the Walnut Street bridge the river has a strong current. In 1 mile it is necessary to portage a low bridge left. After 2¼ miles there is some very fast current as you approach and pass under the third highway crossing, MA 106. One-half mile below, a grassy drag on the right at a culvert is an old farm road that has become so overgrown as to obscure the river downstream. An earth mound affords a view of the extensive meadows. After 1½ miles of more meadows, you reach Maple Street, where the culverts must be portaged.

Below Maple Street (5½ mi) the river flows through a maple swamp, followed by more meadows. Soon the Hockomock empties into the Town River (6¼ mi). Pass under the MA 24 bridge (no access) to the Scotland Street bridge. To reach the river at Scotland Street go east on MA 106 from MA 24. Take the first right (Lincoln Street), bear right onto Elm Street, then bear left onto Scotland Street.

After the Scotland Street bridge (7 mi) the river is wider, deeper, and more sluggish. There is an old stone bridge and three road bridges before you reach the first dam. About ¼ mile below the stone bridge there is a knoll on the right bank that makes a pleasant lunch spot. The Forest Street bridge has been constructed with low supporting trusses and must be carried at high water.

Take out on either side of the dam at War Memorial Park (9½ mi). Access to the park is southwest on River Street from the junction of MA 18 and MA 106. To continue, carry to the main river below the spillway. If the water is too low, put in past the bridge; do not run the canals. There is a rock dam after the bridge, then flatwater for 2½ miles through the marshes to the dam at High Street. To reach the take-out, follow Main Street for one mile past the MA 18/28 and 104 junction and turn right onto High Street.

High Street—MA 104   4 mi

This section is not recommended. The following description is not current. From the High Street dam, portage 100 yards from the right-hand channel across the island and put in below the left-hand dam. Low water may require a longer carry. After 200 yards of quickwater the two channels rejoin. The river is flat as it passes north of Bridgewater in a little valley. Debris in the river becomes more noticeable, especially near a shopping center adjacent to the MA 18 bridge. The river passes under Haywood Street (3 mi) before entering the deadwater at the confluence of the Matfield and Town rivers. Follow the right shore and continue south down the Taunton River for 1/2 mile to the bridge on MA 104 (4 mi).

SATUCKET and MATFIELD RIVERS   MA

The Satucket River flows into the Matfield in East Bridgewater. Both rivers form a part of the Wampanoag Commemorative Canoe Passage. In Bridgewater the Matfield and Town rivers join to form the Taunton River.

The Satucket is a small river that winds past active farms and through woods. Fallen trees can be a problem. The water is clean but dark. The Matfield is a dirty river, and its turbid water is in marked contrast to that of the Satucket at the confluence.

The woods and meadows along the river are very attractive and seemingly isolated, although developing.

Robbins Pond—MA 104   8¹/₄ mi

Description:	Flatwater
Date checked:	1989, JC
Navigable:	Passable at most water levels
Scenery:	Forested, rural, towns
Maps:	USGS Whitman, Bridgewater
Portages:	4¹/₂ mi e dam at Plymouth Street 100 yd

Follow Pond Street northeast from MA 106 to the outlet of Robbins Pond. The Satucket River winds around pastures on the left. Beware of barbed wire and a low bridge. Poor Meadow Brook (1/2 mi) may be passable from MA 27 in Hanson.

After the Washington Street bridge ($1^3/_4$ mi) the river is noticeably wider. Past Bridge Street ($3^1/_4$ mi), where there is good access, the river reaches the backwater of the Plymouth Street Dam. If you can pass under the MA 106 bridge, take out on the left just above the dam and portage past all the buildings. If the water is high, take out on the right, go around the fence 100 yards above the bridge, portage along MA 106 to the right of the factory, and put in from the parking lot.

Below the dam ($4^1/_2$ mi) the river winds in a small wooded valley. After $1^1/_4$ miles the Satucket River flows into the Matfield in a wide marsh. The Matfield enters on the right and is noticeably dirtier. After passing under two bridges, the Matfield goes under some power lines and joins the Town River to form the Taunton River. Past a small dump and a peninsula on the left, the Taunton River flows for $1/_2$ mile south to the MA 104 bridge ($8^1/_4$ mi). It is easy to miss this turn. Take out above the bridge on the right.

NEMASKET RIVER   MA

The Nemasket flows north from a series of ponds in Lakeville through Middleboro to the Taunton River. It is one of the prettiest rivers in eastern Massachusetts. Because Assawompset Pond and its connecting ponds are the water supply for Taunton, the paddler must put in downstream.

Vaugh Street Bridge—Taunton River   11 mi

Description:	Flatwater, quickwater
Date checked:	1989, DS
Navigable:	Passable at all water levels
Scenery:	Forested, rural, towns
Maps:	USGS Assawompset, Bridgewater
Portages:	$3^1/_4$ mi R dams at Municipal Light Plant 50 yd
	$5^1/_4$ mi e dam at Oliver Mill Park (low water) 30 yd

Put in at the Vaugh Street bridge. Vaugh Street is 1.1 miles south of I-495 at exit 4, MA 105, and the bridge is to the left about 1 mile. The river meanders through marshes to the Municipal Light Plant. Do not go under the bridge, but take out on the right, carry across the road, and put in by the fish ladder.

There is ³/₄ mile of quickwater below the dam, then a rocky Class I drop as the river passes through a breach in an old canal wall. The dam at Oliver Mill Park just before the US 44 bridge (5¹/₄ mi) must be carried in low water. The park is an ideal place to put in for easy trips that continue on the Taunton River.

Below US 44 the river winds past a sewage-treatment plant and through forests and marshes for 4¹/₂ miles to the Taunton River. The two bridges, Plymouth Street (7¹/₄ mi) and Murdock Street (8 mi), can be reached by following roads on either side of the river north from US 44. Be careful of the s approach to the Plymouth Street bridge in high water and use the center span. Murdock Street is a fair access point.

There are large meanders under a power line as you approach a railroad bridge and the confluence with the Taunton River (10 mi). The first take-out from the Taunton River is 1 mile downstream at Titicut Street (11 mi), south of the Bridgewater State Prison, and reachable from MA 18/28 via Plymouth Street.

WADING and THREE MILE RIVERS   MA

The Wading River flows from Lake Mirimichi off MA 106 in Foxboro southeast through Mansfield and into Norton, where it meets the Rumford River. At that point, it becomes the Three Mile River, which flows through Taunton. These small, isolated streams wind through woodlands, swamps, and small millponds. There are few houses and buildings near them.

These rivers are passable for a total of 18 miles from Lake Mirimichi to MA 140 just outside Taunton.

The Wading River is a small stream that offers all types of canoeing in early spring (late March), through the summer (some spots will have to be portaged), and usually into the late fall. The area from Barrowsville Pond to the first bridge at MA 140 offers the best canoeing on the river. It is a good spot for the beginning canoeist who lives in the greater Providence area and wants to spend either a whole day or an afternoon paddling on this river, which is forty-five minutes from downtown Providence. It's a popular river with the local paddlers in the spring's high water, although outside of the immediate area it is basically unknown.

Barrowsville Pond—MA 140   3½ mi

Description:	Pond, quickwater, Class, I, II
Date checked:	1985
Navigable:	Medium to high water
Scenery:	Forested, settled, towns
Maps:	USGS Wrentham, Attleboro, Norton
Portage:	½ mi dam at end of pond; low bridge

Starting at Barrowsville Pond, at Power Road, there is a ½-mile paddle across the pond itself to the outlet at the southeastern corner. Portage around the dam. The river then passes under Barrows Road and runs next to a mill on the right. Here the water starts to become quick, and rocks just under the water should be kept in mind. The next ½-mile to a millpond is quick, easy, Class I water. At the millpond are the remains of an old colonial gristmill; the waterway on which the wheel was used has widened sufficiently to create a Class II stretch, which can be run in high water. This rapid should be scouted from the left. This area is a good playing spot that can be portaged back around and run several times before continuing downstream. In high water the waves can become as high as three to four feet, and there is a turn that will require some planning. In low water, this rapid is not recommended, as it becomes scratchy and unrunnable. Directly below is a large pool, with a footbridge that is too low to run and will have to be portaged. The next ½-mile to the chute is just quickwater. Upon reaching the chute, scouting is not usually required (except in low water), as this chute is as straight as an arrow and generally free of obstructions. This is a good run in high water (Class II) and a short portage in low. The next mile to the bridge at MA 140 is easy quickwater, with an occasional fallen tree and midstream boulder. At the bridge at is a 2- to 3-foot ledge, with a midstream boulder directly at the bottom of the chute. This should definitely be scouted. High water makes this boulder difficult to miss, as it is only a canoe's length away from the bottom of the chute. Take-out is possible on the other side of the bridge, just before the gauge station, which is on the left. There is ample parking on either side of the bridge, which is usually fairly full.

MA 140—Taunton River   7 mi

After this point, the river continues through a swamp and becomes overgrown. It is very hard to follow the river as it winds through a maze of trees, and it is definitely not recommended at any time or level. Although the river before MA 140 is fairly clean and the scenery attractive, the stretch below the swamp starts to become noticeably polluted, increasingly so the closer you get to Taunton. The scenery becomes unattractive. The height of ugliness is the sewage treatment plant in Taunton.

COPICUT and SHINGLE ISLAND RIVERS   MA

Map: USGS Fall River East

These two rivers in Dartmouth are part of the drainage of the East Branch of the Westport River. The mile on the Copicut River from Cornell Pond on Hixville Road to the confluence with the Shingle Island River is reported to have been cleared in recent years. The mile on the Shingle Island River below the confluence to Lake Noquochoke is also reported to be open. High water is recommended.

MATTAPOISETT RIVER   MA

The Mattapoisett is a small stream that rises in Snipatuit Pond and flows to Buzzards Bay. The water is very dark, and for most of the distance the river meanders with a good current through brushy swamps. There are occasional houses, farms, and cranberry bogs.

Snipatuit Pond—Mattapoisett   12¹/₄ mi

Description:	Lake, **flatwater,** quickwater,
Date checked:	1989, DS
Navigable:	High water: above MA 105, early spring
	Passable at most water levels: below MA 105
Scenery:	Forested, rural
Maps:	USGS Snipatuit Pond, Marion
Portages:	2³/₄ mi e complex of dams 10 yd
	7³/₄ mi e dam 10 yd

Neck Road in Rochester crosses the north end of Snipatuit Pond, and it is 1³/₄ miles from there to the southeast corner of the pond (to the left of a farm) where the river begins. After about ¹/₄ mile in woods, with numerous windfalls, the stream enters a meadow. This section of the river is not often cleared and involves bushwhacking.

A recommended put-in is at Snipatuit Road (2³/₄ mi), where there is a complex of ponds associated with a fish hatchery. Class I rapids lead to Hartley Road (3¹/₄ mi). The stream is unobstructed as it flows across the bottom of an empty millpond to the remains of Rounseville Dam (4¹/₄ mi), which is runnable at high water.

At MA 105 the river opens up, but soon closes again. The river from here on has enough water to be canoeable all year, if you can stand the brush.

One-and-one-half miles below MA 105 (4¹/₄ mi) you reach Perry Hill Road (5³/₄ mi), and 1¹/₂ miles after that you enter an old millpond. The broken dam is easily run in high water. Below Wolf Island Road (7³/₄ mi), there is a cranberry bog on the right and a dam that must be portaged. The river re-enters the bushes, passes through two old bridge abutments (9³/₄ mi), and finally breaks out into the clear at the Acushnet Road bridge.

The rest is easy. The river passes under I-195, and there are some Class I rapids before you reach a stone bridge (12 mi), a good take-out. The fish weir just above the MA 6 bridge (12¹/₄ mi) can be run, and at low tide there is some quickwater below the bridge.

WEWEANTIC RIVER   MA

The Weweantic River rises in East Carver, provides a portion of the boundary separating Carver and Middleboro, and flows south toward Wareham. It flows through the Great Cedar Swamp and other marshy areas, through heavily wooded areas, and around cranberry bogs.

To reach Popes Point Bridge, take MA 58 south to the first right (Meadow Street), 1 mile south of Carver Center. Take the second right (1 3/4 mi) onto Popes Point Road. From Popes Point Bridge, the course is extremely winding. In 1 1/2 miles, you will come to a pump house at a fork in the river. Go left. In 700 feet you will see power lines. Keep the power lines to the south. This is a very swampy area and the channel is not obvious at high water. Bear left at the fork by the power lines. When portaging the old mill just above the East Street Bridge, be alert for metal spikes. To reach the East Street bridge by car, head southwest on Meadow Street, bearing right to the end. Turn right on Rochester Road to East Street.

Below East Street the river takes a sharp left. There are rocks at low water. The Weweantic is a narrow winding river at this point, with good tree cover. In 1 1/2 miles you come to an old flume with uprights. Go through the middle. You will see cranberry bogs in this area. The river then reaches the MA 58 bridge.

The river passes through cranberry bogs for another mile. Passage is more difficult below the Gibbs Cranberry Bog Dam, and it is only recommended at high water. After 1 1/2 miles you will go under MA 25 and then MA 28. The river then widens and reaches a small pond. Take out at the hydroelectric dam at the end of the pond. To reach the dam's dirt access road, go left on MA 28 from MA 58, then right on Carver Road.

Distances were unavailable for this description. Time estimates provided are 5 to 6 hours from Popes Point to East Street, another 2 1/2 to 3 hours to MA 58, and another 2 1/2 to 3 hours to the hydroelectric dam.

AGAWAM RIVER   MA

This river flows south through cranberry country to Buzzards Bay. It is a small stream with unusually clear water and a fairly dependable flow as it leaves Halfway Pond in Plymouth. This flow is subject to interruption in the fall, however, because the river is dammed in several places to provide water for flooding the cranberry bogs when there is danger of frost.

The first 3½ miles to Glen Charlie Pond are the most attractive. The scenery is varied: cranberry bogs, ponds, pitch pine forests, and a winding stream. Large sections of the two lakes at the end are developed, especially on the east shores.

The river is a delight in November after the cranberry-picking season, when the bogs are a dark maroon color. There are a few places where bogs are right next to the river, and overlooked cranberries can be gathered from the canoe.

Halfway Pond—Wareham   8 mi

Description:	Lakes, flatwater, quickwater, tidal
Date checked:	1985
Navigable:	High or medium water: spring and fall
Scenery:	Forested, rural, settled
Maps:	USGS Sagamore, Wareham
Portages:	1/4 mi R low bridge 10 yd
	1/2 mi L diversion dam 20 yd
	1¼ mi L reservoir dam 20 yd
	3¼ mi L dam on Stump Lake 10 yd
	5 mi L dam on Glen Charlie Pond 10 yd
	5¼ mi R dam 10 yd
	7 mi R dam on Mill Pond 20 yd

Begin at Halfway Pond, which is east of Myles Standish State Forest in Plymouth. The river leaves the south end of the pond, and in 200 yards, passes a dirt road. Soon there is a small cranberry bog on the right, and then the first carry. In a short distance the stream passes through a cranberry bog for ½ mile, requiring a carry around a diversion dam. At the end of the bog (¾ mi), the canoe must be dragged over boards in a large culvert. Soon the stream opens into a reservoir.

Below the reservoir dam (1^1/$_4$ mi) there is another large cranberry bog that extends along the river for ^{3}/$_4$ miles. Then there is a very nice ^{1}/$_2$-mile quickwater run through an open pitch pine forest. Just before you enter Stump Lake (2^1/$_2$ mi) there is an old bridge that canoes can be dragged over.

Stump Lake has many surprises just below the surface. In spite of the crystal-clear water, the submerged stumps are not easy to spot. Below the dam (3^1/$_4$ mi) a short stretch of quickwater leads to Glen Charlie Pond. Pass a number of houses and a wide bay on the left, and continue more or less straight to the dam (5 mi).

Shortly after Glen Charlie Pond there is another dam (5^1/$_4$ mi), some quickwater, then Mill Pond. Follow the left shore as the lake winds for over 1^1/$_2$ miles to the dam.

At the end of Mill Pond (7 mi), carry across the westbound lane of US 6/MA 28 and run quickwater past the bridge carrying the eastbound lane, below which you reach tidewater. The river swings to the right through salt marshes and passes under US 6 (8 mi), just pass which there is good access on the right.

BASS RIVER   MA

The Bass offers diverse scenery along its route. From its mouth at West Dennis Beach, it passes north into a series of wide ponds separated by narrows. In the ponds canoes will be influenced by southwest winds. In the narrows, paddlers contend with short stretches of tidal current. At the mouth, saltbox houses give way to moored yachts. The middle section is bordered by conservation land, some of the last undeveloped property on the Cape. The uppermost pond offers warm-water swimming by mid-May.

West Dennis Beach—Mill Pond   7 mi

Description:	Flatwater, quickwater, tidal
Date checked:	1989, GE
Navigable:	All year
Scenery:	Settled, forested, marsh, cranberry bogs
Map:	USGS Dennis

A southwest wind will help paddlers putting in at the mouth and paddling to Mill Pond. It is also advisable to put in 1 or 2 hours before high tide. High tide at the mouth is 1 hour after high tide in Boston.

Put in on the west side of the Loring Avenue culvert next to the West Dennis Beach traffic circle. Park by the side of the rotary, or in the Beach parking area. Boat launching from the Beach is prohibited. This section runs west between residential docks and low sand dunes before turning right into the main channel. Paddling north toward the tall MA 28 brige (2 mi) you'll see how well you judged the wind and tide. Under the bridge, the Bass slackens as it enters the first of six wide areas. After passing the dead-end cove on the right, paddle straight ahead toward the Bass River Country Club (2$\frac{1}{2}$ mi). Take the channel on you right, keeping the Country Club on your left as you enter the second and largest wide area.

Here you can explore Grand Cove on your right, adding 2$\frac{1}{2}$ miles to your trip, or proceed with Salt Box Beach on the left to a sharp left bend past a public landing (good access) and under the Great Western Road bridge (3$\frac{1}{2}$ mi). By logic fathomable only to New Englanders, you have now reached South Dennis by paddling north from West Dennis. The town conservation land on the right, $\frac{1}{2}$ before the US 6 bridge (4$\frac{1}{2}$ mi), is a superb picnic spot. A large rock in the river has a cylindrical hole in it, which natives claim was used by the Vikings as a mooring. It is known that Indians used this area as a fishing village.

From here the Bass constricts into its 500-yard-long narrows, where tidal influence is greatest. Tides here are four hours later than at the mouth. Current under the US 6 bridge forms 3-foot standing waves twice a day, halfway between high and low tides, which weaken to nothing at full high and low. Timing this trip as indicated above will ensure that a current favors passage here.

Above US 6 (4$\frac{1}{2}$ mi) tidal influence is minimal. The Bass widens into Kelleys Bay on the right, and Dinahs Pond on the left. Continue by taking the channel between them. Another constriction leads to Follins Pond (5$\frac{1}{4}$ mi). Keep to the left shore until the pond is behind you and a creek that forks (6 mi) is ahead. The narrow channel on the right leads to Mill Pond. Avoid the wider channel on the left, which soon ends in a small pond.

The right channel leads to a shallow creek that passes through a stone-lined culvert under North Dennis Road (6¼ mi). The culvert is narrow enough to allow paddlers to grip both walls and pull the canoe through. The upper reaches of the Bass take on a wilderness quality. The quiet backwater slowly opens up into Mill Pond, which is far enough from the ocean to contain very little salt. Its dark waters and shallow bottom make Mill Pond one of the first warm swimming spots of the year. Outward Reach Road (7 mi) comes down to the pond shore on the right, making an ideal take-out.

SCORTON CREEK   MA

Ploughed Neck Road—Scorton Neck   4 mi

Description:	Tidal
Date checked:	1989, CC
Map:	USGS Sandwich

Put in at the mouth of the creek at Cape Cod Bay. Go ¹/₁₀ mile east of the railroad crossing on MA 6A, north on Ploughed Neck Road for ⁸/₁₀ mile to North Shore Boulevard, and right almost to the end of the road. Turn right between cottages to the put-in. Parking is limited.

For an alternate put-in, go south of the MA 6A bridge, and east of Ploughed Neck Road via the former State Bird Farm entrance. You will be fighting the tide if you put in here. There are sand bars at the bridge at low tide.

Do not plan on crossing the dunes to the beach. Pull up canoes on the east shore of the creek mouth and walk around to the end of the dunes.

There are 4 miles of creek to explore, with good birding and salmon fishing.

Chapter 7

Atlantic Coastal Watersheds

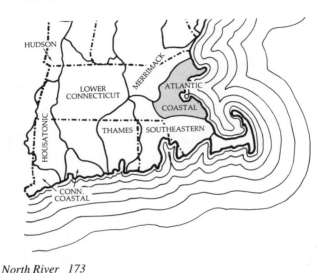

ATLANTIC COASTAL WATERSHEDS

The rivers in this section drain eastern Massachusetts and flow eastward to the Atlantic Ocean. Due to their proximity to population centers, the most desirable sections are heavily used, and efforts are being made by both public and private agencies to protect their scenic attractiveness and recreational access. The canoeing season on them is long. Only the Drinkwater and Indian Head rivers, written as part of the North River, require high water for easy passage.

Good rapids, though short, are to be found at all seasons at the Cohasset Tidal Rips. There are some rapids on the Drinkwater and Indian Head rivers, but they are not likely to satisfy a whitewater enthusiast's desire.

In addition, two sections of tidewater not associated with the rivers are included, as they seemed to have special merit for canoeists.

NORTH RIVER   MA

- This river has a freshwater and a tidal section. Under the name of Drinkwater River, it flows south in the western part of Hanover; as the Indian Head River it runs eastward forming the boundary between Hanover and Hanson. The tidal portion is called the North River. The Drinkwater and Indian Head rivers require high water; the North River is passable at high or low tide, with high tide preferred.

The upper rivers are contrasts of unspoiled woods and growing suburbs, of quiet millponds and commercial districts, of clean water and discarded junk. The tidal North River, which is being considered for protection under the state's Scenic Rivers Act, is the most attractive part of the river system.

West Hanover—MA 3A   **15³/₄ mi**

Description:	Lakes, Flatwater, Class I-II; **Tidal**
Date checked:	1989, HS (North River only—upper section not current)
Navigable:	High water: recommended for freshwater sections, early spring
	Medium water: scratchy in freshwater sections, spring and late fall
Scenery:	Forested, settled
Maps:	USGS Whitman, Hanover, Cohasset, Scituate
Portages:	1¹/₄ mi L 2nd King St. bridge 30 yd
	2³/₄ mi R dam on Factory Pond 10 yd
	4 mi L dam in South Hanover 100 yd
	5¹/₂ mi e dam at Elm St. 30 yd

Put in from MA 139 in West Hanover. After King Street (¹/₂ mi) there is ¹/₄ mile of Class II rapids that are scratchy in medium water. At the second King Street crossing (1¹/₄ mi) there is a bridge that may have to be portaged because of low clearance in high water.

The dam at the outlet of Forge Pond can be run, and it leads to a narrow, shallow Class II rapid. Halfway down at an old bridge there is a dam with a 1-foot drop that can be lined.

There is a bridge across Factory Pond just before it hooks around to the left. Portage the dam (2³/₄ mi) on the right beside the factory. Flatwater continues as the stream passes under a bridge and through a swampy area with some small, passable debris dams. At the South Hanover dam (4 mi), take out at the culvert on the left if the water is high.

Below the dam in South Hanover there are 100 yards of Class II rapids, with flatwater for ¹/₄ mile to a shorter Class II drop that is runnable if not blocked. After another ¹/₂ mile of mostly flatwater there is a Class II drop at an old damsite beside a factory up on the left bank. The river soon enters the deadwater behind the dam at Elm Street, where there is good access.

Below Elm Street (5¹/₂ mi) the Indian Head River enters the tidal marshes. There is good access from Riverside Drive about ¹/₄ mile below Elm Street. After a short distance the Indian Head River joins Herring Creek to form the North River. The lower sections of the North River are subject to a strong tidal current. At its mouth the tides are the same as Boston, but upstream it turns as much as three hours later at the MA 53 bridge in Hanover.

The North River snakes for 10¹/₂ miles to Massachusetts Bay. It is continuously bordered by marshes, and several markers identify the sites of colonial shipyards. There are five highway crossings between Elm Street and the ocean. The first two are MA 53/139 and, a few hundred yards farther, Washington Street in Hanover. Access is difficult at these bridges. The next crossing is MA 3 (no access). About 1 mile below MA 3 is a nice picnic spot at Blueberry Island on the south side of the river. The next highway crossing is Bridge Street in Norwell, where there is good access. The final bridge is MA 3A (15³/₄ mi) where there is access through marinas. A final access is available from the Driftway in Scituate about ³/₄ mile back up the First Herring Brook on your left, about 1 mile below MA 3A.

The open ocean is 1³/₄ miles below MA 3A at New Inlet, where the North and South rivers meet and flow into the ocean. There are very strong tidal currents in New Inlet, which may present a hazard, especially with an outgoing tide and a strong offshore breeze.

COHASSET TIDAL RIPS   MA

Situated between Cohasset Harbor and The Gulf, this is a place frequently used for whitewater instruction and practice by canoeists and kayakers. It is located on the south side of Cohasset Harbor just below the Border Street bridge and near the restaurant Hugo's Lighthouse.

Beginning at high tide, the water flows out for nine hours. As the level of Cohasset Harbor drops, a short, narrow, and turbulent rapid is exposed. At its most difficult stage, near low tide, it is Class VI and too rough for open canoes. Kayakers attempting it must know what they are doing, for there is a danger of both boat and body getting injured on the ledges.

The best conditions for practice in canoes begin when the rapids reverse midway on the incoming tide. Within the 3 hours preceding high tide, the rapids build up to a wide Class II pitch with heavy waves and strong eddies. The current begins to lessen about 1 hour before high tide, when the flow reverses again. Tide times are about the same as Boston.

BOSTON HARBOR ISLANDS   MA

Boston Harbor contains 30 islands, many of them owned publicly and administered by the Metropolitan District Commission (MDC) and the Department of Environmental Management (DEM).

The islands feature seashell beaches, historic forts, hiking paths, birds and wildlife, and flowering meadows. During the summer months special programs are run on many of the islands.

Ferry service is available from Long Wharf and Rowes Wharf in Boston as well as from Hingham, Hull, and Lynn. The ferries are privately owned and charge a small fee. The DEM runs a free water taxi from Georges Island to five other islands for easy island hopping.

In addition, Hingham Bay is sufficiently sheltered so that islands are easily accessible to paddlers in moderate weather and most stages of the tide.

Contact the MDC (617-727-5290) or the DEM (617-740-1605) for more information about the islands, special programs, or camping permits.

NEPONSET RIVER   MA

The Neponset flows from Foxboro to Dorchester Bay. Many old mills are located along the river, especially in Walpole. The river is passable all year below Norwood. The Neponset Watershed Association, 293 Hill Street, Sharon, MA 02067, is working to improve the quality of the river and has a folder on canoeing information.

Norwood—Hyde Park   9¹/₂ mi

Description:	**Flatwater,** Class I
Date checked:	1989, DH
Navigable:	High and medium water: January through May and after heavy rain
	Passable at all water levels below exit 11 off I-95
Scenery:	Forested, settled, urban
Maps:	USGS Norwood, Blue Hills

The attractive section of the river ends at the Neponset Valley Parkway at historic Paul's Bridge. You can continue on under Paul's Bridge to the Hallingsworth Dam. Access beyond this point is impossible due to fencing; if you go to the dam you must paddle upstream to Paul's Bridge. This is not recommended.

CHARLES RIVER   MA

The Charles River is the major recreational waterway in the Boston area. The winding, 80-mile river passes many towns, offering some good canoeing, sailing, fishing, and picnic areas for a large population.

Clean-up campaigns, storm-drain diversion projects, and tighter pollution laws have all helped to make the Charles a cleaner river. The water, however, will always be dark. The brown color is primarily due to tannins contained in surrounding border vegetation and is not a sign of pollution. The nearly twenty dams and ninety-odd bridges have slowed the flow of the river so that it cannot flush itself. In the summer the water tends to stagnate behind the dams, but they do help to maintain canoeable water level throughout the season.

The Army Corps of Engineers has preserved 8,500 acres of floodplain as part of a floodplain-management system. The Metropolitan District Commission is active in the recreational development of the lower 40 miles of the river, and have published a folder detailing their many recreational facilities on the Charles and other local waterways. This is free from MDC Headquarters, 20 Somerset Street, Boston, MA 02108.

The Charles River Watershed Association (2391 Commonwealth Avenue, Auburndale, MA 02166) is a nonprofit organization dedicated to the welfare of the river. They publish *The Charles River Canoe Guide* and furnish information about conservation activities in the watershed.

North Bellingham—MA 109   14¹/2 mi

Description:	**Flatwater,** Class I-II
Date checked:	1989, DL, JD'A
Navigable:	High water: recommended above MA 115, March, April
	Medium water: rapids above MA 115 bony, late April to June, fall
	Low water: some spots thin below MA 115
Scenery:	Forested, rural, settled
Maps:	USGS Franklin, Holliston, Medfield
Portages:	1¹/4 mi R Caryville Dam
	3¹/4 mi R dam
	5¹/4 mi L Medway Dam (difficult) 200 yd

The portion of the Charles starting at Medway is especially recommended. There are occasional rapids in an attractive setting, with mostly woods and meadows with an occasional house. There are no portages in this section.

The source of the Charles is north of Echo Lake in Hopkinton. The river above North Bellingham is small and steep in some sections; other sections are fenced-in and unattractive. At one of the crossings of I-495, passage is not possible in high water, and the area is fenced, making portage impossible.

In Medway, put in from the bridge on Sanford Street (Lincoln Street in Franklin), which crosses Village Street next to a convenience store in Medway.

In North Bellingham, begin on the left bank from the parking lot behind a mill on Maple Street. There are some Class I rapids at the start. In 1¹/4 miles you reach a small pond behind a dam. Carry right.

In 2 miles there is another pond and dam, with the third dam 2 miles beyond that.

Medway Dam (5¹/₄ mi) should be portaged on the left. Carry past the industrial buildings through a new parking lot, cross Sanford Street, and carry down 200 yards to the end of River Street to a break in the guardrail, on the right. Carry across a shallow canal and an island to the river.

Immediately below the Sanford Street bridge (5¹/₄ mi), the river enters a steep valley where there are some easy Class II rapids. Part way down there is an old, washed-out, runnable dam. The current slackens to flatwater at the Populatic Street bridge (5¹/₂ mi), where there is good access. After 1¹/₂ miles the river enters Populatic Lake (7 mi). Follow the left shore 200 yards to the outlet.

Below Populatic Lake the river is noticeably wider and deeper. After 1¹/₄ miles Mill River (8¹/₄ mi) enters on the right through a culvert. The Mill may be canoed in high water for 2 miles, from just below City Mills Pond off Main Street in Norfolk. After the Mill River culvert there is easy access on the right bank from River Road.

Just beyond the Mill River there are Class I rapids at the Myrtle Street Bridge. Passage under the left span is recommended, as the right span has submerged boulders. Rockville Rips (8³/₄ mi) at the Pleasant Street bridge in Millis begin at a broken dam with narrow channels that require quick maneuvering. The left is recommended at high water; the right at medium water. The bridge is fifteen feet downstream. The left and center spans offer clear passage, but the right contains submerged boulders. Quickwater is followed by flatwater to the MA 115 bridge.

Below the MA 115 bridge (9¹/₂ mi) there is a short section of quickwater. Passage is left of center. The remaining 5 miles to MA 109 are mostly flat, with meadows lining one or both of the banks. The Forest Street bridge (11 mi) provides good access.

The Stop River enters at 13³/₄ miles. In high or medium water it is canoeable for 2¹/₂ miles from South Street in Medfield.

MA 109—Needham   16¹/₂ mi

Description:	Flatwater
Date checked:	1989, JD'A
Navigable:	Navigable at all water levels
Scenery:	Forested, settled, urban
Maps:	USGS Medfield, Natick
Portages:	10¹/₂ mi R South Natick Dam
	(16¹/₂ mi) Cochrane Dam

One of the best parts of the river is above South Natick Dam, offering a large bird population including heron and owls. Large meadows in Medfield and Millis give way to wooded banks and smaller meadows in Dover and Sherborn. Land on the north side at Rocky Narrows is owned by the Trustees of Reservations. In Natick, the river borders the Massachusetts Audubon Society's Broadmoor Sanctuary. The river meanders in the large meadow between MA 109 and MA 27, making the wind a factor. The section between Broadmoor Sanctuary and South Natick Dam can be scratchy in low water.

There are many sharp meanders past the mouth of Bogastow Brook (2¹/₂ mi) on the left to the MA 27 bridge (3¹/₂ mi), where access may be gained from the southbound lane. In 2 miles the river passes through Rocky Narrows, an interesting feature. The ledge on the right bank offers a nice view and pleasant lunch spot. In 1¹/₂ miles the Bridge Street bridge (7 mi), where there is good access, is reached. Take out on the right at the South Natick Dam (10¹/₂ mi) in a small park area.

Put in on the right from the Coatings Engineering parking lot (10¹/₂ mi). In the next few miles the river wanders erratically, so a map is handy. After 5¹/₂ miles there is a road bridge followed closely by a railroad bridge. Take out on the left at an MDC parking area just above the dam (16¹/₂ mi) at South Street in Charles River Village, Needham.

Needham—Norumbega Park   18¹/₄ mi

Description:	**Flatwater,** Class II
Date checked:	1989, DL
Navigable:	Navigable at all water levels, except at beginning
Scenery:	Forested, urban
Maps:	USGS Natick, Newton
Portages:	13¹/₂ mi L Silk Mill Dam
	13³/₄ mi R Metropolitan Circular Dam
	15¹/₂ mi L Cordingly Dam
	15³/₄ mi L Finlay Dam

Put in below Cochrane Dam, which is at the west end of South Street in Needham. In high water there are 400 yards of Class II rapids below the dam, which are often used for whitewater training. If the water is low, or if you want a flatwater trip, put in downstream. At the Chestnut Street bridge (1¹/₂ mi) there are more, short rapids that are shallow in low water.

Below Chestnut Street in Needham, the Charles flows generally eastward and passes under MA 135 (3 mi) and MA 128 (I-95). Soon it swings in a big loop through Dedham. The Dedham Loop can be bypassed by following Long Ditch, which leaves on the left below MA 128 and rejoins the Charles at the railroad bridge below Dedham. It is ³/₄ mile long and cuts off 5¹/₄ miles of river.

Below the lower end of Long Ditch (9³/₄) the river flows through an attractive marsh before it reaches the industrial area above the two dams in Newton Upper Falls. Portage the first one (13¹/₂ mi) across the grassy area on the left and put in before Echo Bridge. Portage the second (13³/₄ mi) on the right and carry down Quinobequin Road under MA 9.

The 1¹/₂ miles from Newton Upper Falls to Newton Lower Falls are close to MA 128. Cordingly Dam (15¹/₂ mi) is portaged on the left through the parking lot of the Walnut Street industrial area. At the put-in there are a few whitewater rips, and they are followed in a few hundred yards by the Finlay Dam, which must be carried on the left over the street.

It is 2¹/₂ miles from Newton Lower Falls past MA 128 to the MA 30 bridge (18¹/₄ mi) at Norumbega.

Norumbega Park—Charles River Dam   14³/₄ mi

Description:	Lakes, **flatwater**
Date checked:	1989, DL, JH
Navigable:	Navigable at all water levels
Maps:	USGS Natick, Newton, Boston South
Portages:	2³/₄ mi R Moody St. Dam 300 yd
	3³/₄ mi R Bleachery Dam 100 yd
	5³/₄ mi R Watertown Dam 50 yd

Just below the intersection of MA 128 (I-95) and the Massachusetts Turnpike (I-90), the Charles widens into an impoundment formed by the Moody Street Dam. The scenery in this area is as beautiful as any to be found on the river. Unfortunately, traffic noise and motorboats are an intrusion.

A historic point of interest in this section is the stone tower on a hill in the Charles River Reservation about ¹/₂ mile below the put-in. Although placed to mark the spot where Norseman supposedly settled in 1543, subsequent research has disproven the theory.

The put-in may be reached by following the signs to MA 30 from MA 128 or the Massachusetts Turnpike and then by following the signs to the duck-feeding station across from the Marriott Hotel. The put-in is at the extreme left. An alternate put-in is available at Recreation Road off MA 128. The Charles River Canoe and Kayak Club offers rentals at the put-in.

The river narrows dramatically at the Prospect Street bridge (2 mi), below which the banks become more urban. Take out on the right at the Moody Street Dam (2³/₄ mi). Carry across Moody Street and across the bridge to Riverbend Park. Follow the path and put in below the footbridge.

The Bleachery Dam (3³/₄ mi), which lies 100 yards below a wooden railroad bridge, can be lined under certain conditions. If portage is necessary, carry 100 yards along the right bank. The Rolling Stone Dam (4³/₄ mi) has been breached and can be run easily on the left. A short stretch of quickwater follows. The Watertown Dam ($5^3/4$ mi) is marked by a modern, steel-beam footbridge that lies forty yards upstream. The dam is easily portaged on the right.

Below the Galen Street bridge in Watertown (6 mi) the Charles begins to widen. Traffic increases in this area. It is possible to paddle the entire basin, through the locks ($14^3/4$ mi), and out into Boston Harbor.

MYSTIC RIVER   MA

The Mystic River flows from Upper Mystic Lake in Winchester roughly southeast to the ocean. It is short, easily canoeable, and flat. The upper river is urban but generally pleasant; the tidal portion is heavily industrial, polluted, and filled with heavy shipping. For further information, contact the Mystic River Watershed Association, 276 Massachusetts Avenue, Apt. #510, Arlington, MA 02174.

Mystic Lakes—Boston Harbor   9 mi

Description:	Flatwater, tidal
Date checked:	1988, GE
Navigable:	Passable at all water levels
Scenery:	Settled, urban
Maps:	USGS Lexington, Boston North
Portage:	$1^1/4$ mi R dam

In high or medium water it is possible to start on the Aberjona River and paddle about 1 mile from Winchester Center to Mystic Lake, with a carry around the USGS weir. Usually the Mystic Lakes will provide a better start.

From the entrance of the Aberjona River into Upper Mystic Lake at its northeast corner, it is about $1^1/4$ miles south to Lower Mystic Lake; portage right through the Medford Boat Club facilities. It is then $1/2$ mile to the river's exit at the southeast corner of Lower Mystic Lake. In $1/4$ mile the MA 60 bridge (2 mi) is passed, and in another $^1/_2$ mile the Harvard Avenue bridge is passed. Alewife Brook enters on the right in another 500 yards.

In the next mile the Mystic River is largely contained by parkways. It passes beneath seven bridges before it reaches Medford Center (4 mi). Be careful of motorboats in this area. Below Medford Center is the basin formed by the Amelia Earhart Dam in Everett. An expanded greenbelt lines the river.

The Malden River enters just above the dam; it is broad with marshes, two small undeveloped islands, and commercial development. It can be paddled for $1^3/_4$ mi.

Bring a boat horn. At Amelia Earhart Dam give two long and two short blasts to be put through the lock into the tidal part of the river. In $2^1/_2$ miles pass under the Mystic-Tobin Bridge and see Old Ironsides and the Charlestown Naval Shipyard National Park. The Charles River enters on the right and you are in Boston Harbor (9 mi).

LITTLE RIVER and ALEWIFE BROOK   MA

Little River is a small, seldom-visited stream with more wildlife than would be expected in such an urban setting. Alewife Brook, which connects Little River to the Mystic River, is not recommended.

Little Pond—Mystic River $2^1/_2$ mi

Description:	Flatwater
Date checked:	1989, GE
Navigable:	Passable at most water levels
Scenery:	Urban
Map:	Boston North

The put-in is at Little Pond, accessible by a public trail (50 yd) off Brighton Street between Larch Circle and Sandrick Road in Belmont. The river leaves the middle of the eastern shore. The beginning of the trip has forested banks that soon give way to an industrial park. The Little River goes under a footbridge (1 mi), then under the MA 2 bridge to join Alewife Brook. Alewife Brook is flanked by concrete banks and a hurricane fence, and littered by shopping carts. The trash level has improved since 1985, and the entire length of the waterway can be safely negotiated.

IPSWICH RIVER   MA

The Ipswich River winds from Burlington to the ocean near the south end of Plum Island. It runs through many miles of wetlands in an area dotted with drumlins and other glacial formations.

Housing developments and urban areas are scattered all along the river, but they are separated by long sections of woods, swamps, and meadows. In particular, the $8^3/_4$-mile section from I-95 eastward through Bradley Palmer State Park is especially attractive because large segments of the river corridor are protected by the Audubon Society and local, county, and state agencies, as well as through easements obtained by the Essex County Greenbelt Association.

From source to mouth there is a varying amount of debris in and along the river. The section along MA 62 in North Reading is the most cluttered.

Wilmington—Howe Station   12$^1/_2$ mi

Description:	Flatwater
Date checked:	1985
Navigable:	Passable at most water levels
Scenery:	Forested, settled
Maps:	USGS Wilmington, Reading, Salem
Portage:	7$^1/_4$ mi L dam in Peabody 20 yd

The going is slow in this section, with wide meanders, alders, fallen trees, and many small bridges. Ducks and other birds are much in evidence.

Put in from the bridge on Woburn Street, which parallels I-93 west of exit 27 (Concord Street). The river is very small as it passes through Hundred Acre Swamp before I-93 ($^1/_2$ mi). Then it winds for 7 miles, passing under Haverhill Street in North Reading (4$^1/_2$ mi) about halfway to the dam in Peabody. Then the river becomes more isolated as it flows in wide wetlands past the MA 114 bridge ($10\frac{1}{4}$ mi). There is good access at the MA 62 bridge ($12\frac{1}{2}$ mi).

Howe Station—Willowdale Dam $11\frac{3}{4}$ mi

Description:	Flatwater, quickwater
Date checked:	1985
Navigable:	Passable at most water levels
Scenery:	Forested, settled
Maps:	USGS Georgetown, Ipswich
Portage:	($11\frac{3}{4}$ mi R Willowdale Dam)

This is the most popular section of the Ipswich River for canoeing, with a fair current and many meanders. The river flows under several bridges, among them I-95 (3 mi), US 1 ($5\frac{1}{4}$ mi), and MA 97 ($6\frac{1}{4}$ mi), before it reaches Wenham Swamp. As it does, (just after a railroad bridge), the Salem-Beverly Waterway Canal leaves on the right. In very high water the river may be difficult to follow through Wenham Swamp.

The river turns north through an area where the shores are protected. Nature trails wander along the left bank. Where the river swings east again, the valley narrows. Take out on the left where the river comes close to Topsfield Road.

Willowdale Dam—Ipswich   5 mi

Description:	Flatwater, Class I
Date checked:	1985
Navigable:	Passable at most water levels
Scenery:	Forested, settled
Map:	USGS Ipswich
Portage:	(5 mi L dam)

Put in at the bridge just downstream of Willowdale Dam. Most of the distance is flat and deep, but some shallow spots and rock dams may require wading/lining at low water. At the first bridge ($^1/_2$ mi), debris collects on a row of rocks. After another $1^1/_4$ miles there is a rocky ledge. Below the next bridge shallow riffles continue for $^1/_2$ mile to the ponding from the dam in Ipswich.

This 3-foot dam is upstream of the southbound MA 1A bridge. It is entirely confined within vertical retaining walls and cannot be portaged at the site. A public canoe access is upstream on the left above the walls.

Paddling upstream from this ramp is feasible.

Ipswich—Atlantic Ocean   3$^1/_2$ mi

The dam is approximately the head of the tide. In low water, the river below is shallow at low tide. Access immediately below the dam is impractical, but there is a boat ramp on the north side 1 mile downstream. Wind can be a problem as the river widens, with salt marshes along the edge. In favorable weather on a rising tide, one can paddle north inside Plum Island to the mouth of the Merrimack. The tidal difference is $8^1/_2$ to 10 feet, with high tide about the same as Boston and low tide twenty minutes later.

PARKER RIVER   MA

The Parker rises in Groveland and is freshwater until Central Street in Byfield, where it becomes tidal. The freshwater section is canoeable between Crane Pond in Groveland and River Road in Byfield Center. The freshwater section can be canoed in either direction. Crane Pond is reached from a small road off Thurlow Street in Georgetown. Put in on River Road, off Forest Street, where the road crosses a power line. The gate is intended for trailbikers, not paddlers; put in 20 feet up the right-of-way.

Georgetown—Byfield   2¹/₂ mi

Description:	Lake, **flatwater**
Date checked:	1989, MS
Navigable:	Passable at most water levels
Scenery:	Forested, towns
Maps:	USGS Georgetown, Newburyport West, Newburyport East

From Crane Pond the river flows 1¹/₂ miles through meadows, then passes through steep banks of hemlocks. Shortly the river widens into a millpond at the power line. This is the take-out.

The tidal section of the Parker is passable from Central Street, Byfield, for 9 miles to the Plum River. This section is best paddled three hours before and three hours after high tide, which is a little later than Boston. Access is available at Middle Road north of Governor Dummer Academy in Byfield, on MA 1A in Newbury at the town landing (resident sticker required), and US 1 in Newbury.

PLUM RIVER   MA

The Plum offers a protected passage from the Merrimack River mouth behind Plum Island to the Ipswich River. The Parker River enters from the west roughly at the halfway point.

Merrimack River—Ipswich River   8 mi

Description:	Tidal
Date checked:	1989, MS
Maps:	USGS Newburyport East, Ipswich

Access is available at the Plum Island Turnpike bridge, from MA 1A on the Parker, or from the Ipswich beaches. The tide on the Plum River from the Plum Island bridge to the Parker (4 mi) is not strong: it is possible to paddle against the tide. The best time to paddle this section is within 3 hours of high tide, which is a little later than

Boston. This section passes through the Parker River National Wildlife Refuge.

It is possible to begin a trip on the Parker at the beginning of the outgoing tide and paddle up the Plum before the tide gets too low.

The tide on the lower Plum and on the Parker is very strong and difficult to boat against. **Caution!** The current can be dangerous. Skilled paddlers can begin a trip at the north end, paddle the outgoing tide to the Ipswich beaches, and beat the tide. You must wait at least an hour after the tide turns to begin the return trip on the incoming tide.

Chapter 8

Merrimack Watershed

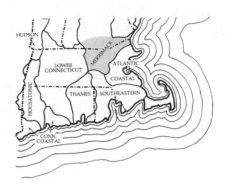

MERRIMACK WATERSHED

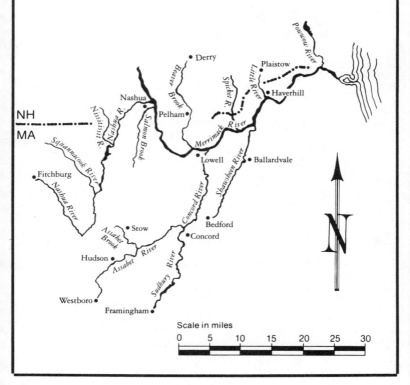

Derry

Plaistow

Powwow River

Spicket R.

Little River

Haverhill

Nashua

Beaver Brook

Pelham

NH
MA

Nissitissit R.

Nashua R.

Salmon Brook

Merrimack River

Squannacook River

Lowell

Shawsheen River

Ballardvale

Fitchburg

Nashua River

Concord River

Assabet Brook

Stow

Bedford

Concord

Hudson

Assabet River

Sudbury River

Westboro

Framingham

N

Scale in miles

0   5   10   15   20   25   30

The Merrimack Watershed dominates central New Hampshire and northeastern Massachusetts. It encompasses, and is situated next to, large population centers; sections of rivers throughout the watershed are heavily paddled.

The Merrimack is already a large river when it crosses into Massachusetts. Many of its frequently canoed tributaries lie in New Hampshire and are described in the New Hampshire/Vermont River Guide. *Only tributaries that flow at least in part through Massachusetts are described in this book. Since, however, all-the-way-down-the-Merrimack trips are becoming more common, the entire main stem description is included.*

Further information about the river can be obtained from the Merrimack River Watershed Council, 694 Main Street, West Newbury, MA 01935.

MERRIMACK RIVER   NH, MA

The Merrimack River begins in Franklin, New Hampshire, at the confluence of the Pemigewasset and Winnipesaukee rivers. It flows south into Massachusetts and then turns east and runs into the sea at Newburyport.

Except in the large cities, the banks are still rather nice from a distance. Suburban sprawl usually does not reach the river's edge. From Franklin to Concord, the river has a sandy bottom. The closer you get to the sea, the muddier and more polluted the river becomes.

Almost all of the river is runnable throughout the paddling season. It should be avoided at high water, however, when the current is fast; the landings are difficult and the approaches to the dams are dangerous.

Most of the big drops have been harvested for power. When the river's natural flow is low, the water level is affected by the demand for electricity. Low water has the biggest impact on the paddler below Franklin and below Amoskeag Dam in Manchester. Information on daily flows can be obtained by calling the dispatcher at the Public Service Company of New Hampshire (603-225-6182).

The Merrimack is close to many large population centers, and launching ramps provide access to all sections of the river.

In Penacook, at the mouth of the Contoocook River, sits Hannah Duston Island. It was there that Hannah Duston, who was captured by Indians in a raid in Haverhill, Massachusetts, on March 15, 1697, a week after the birth of her eighth child, escaped her captors. On the morning of March 31, with the help of Mary Neff, who had been taken prisoner at the same time, and a youth who had been captured in a raid in Worcester, Massachusetts, Hannah killed and scalped ten of the twelve Indians guarding her. The other two fled, and the three prisoners went downriver by canoe to Nashua. Hannah later received a bounty of 25 pounds per scalp from the Massachusetts General Court.

Franklin—Concord   24 mi

Description:	Flatwater, quickwater, Class I
Date checked:	1988, WF
Navigable:	Passable at all water levels
	Dam controlled, peak power generation on Pemigewasset River
Scenery:	Forested, settled
Maps:	USGS Penacook 15, Concord

Put in on the Pemigewasset River below Eastman Falls Dam if you want to begin with 1 mile of Class II rapids. If you prefer $1/2$ mile of quickwater, begin on the Winnepesaukee River behind the high school in Franklin.

From the confluence of the Pemigewasset and Winnepesaukee rivers, there are Class I rapids for the first $1/2$ mile. Then there is a moderate current to Boscawen ($10^1/2$ mi), where the first bridge (closed) is located. Another $4^1/2$ miles of meandering river bring you to Penacook, the US 4 bridge off exit 17 of I-93 (poor access), and the mouth of the Contoocook River on the right.

In the mouth of the Contoocook River (15 mi) there is an island joined to the mainland by two railroad bridges, which are a monument to Hannah Duston. In 2 miles there is another bridge with a launching ramp downstream on the right. From that point it is 1 mile to Sewall Falls Dam, which has been breached and no longer needs to be portaged. Beware of assorted debris and a new set of standing waves now rated as Class III. Consider scouting the run. A nice sand beach on the right shore just above the dam offers a fine landing place. The dam itself is old, and care should be taken when using it as a vantage point.

Below Sewall Falls Dam (18 mi) there is a Class III rapid that is ¹/₄ mile long and rocky in low water. In another 3¹/₂ miles there is a railroad bridge and an I-93 bridge. Just upstream from this is a launching ramp that can be reached from exit 16. The remaining distance to the Bridge Street bridge (24 mi) was shortened in 1976 when a new channel was cut across a meander. A new launching ramp is on the right bank near the cloverleaf of I-393, 1 mile above Bridge Street.

Concord—Manchester   18¹/₄ mi

Description:	Flatwater, quickwater
Date checked:	1988, WO
Navigable:	Passable at all water levels
	Dam controlled, good flow all year
Scenery:	Forested, settled
Maps:	USGS Concord 15, Suncook, Manchester North
Portages:	5 mi L Garvin's Falls Dam 100 yd
	10¹/₂ mi L dam at Hooksett ¹/₄ mi
	(18¹/₄ mi R Amoskeag Dam 200 yd)

There are boat-launching ramps just above the Bridge Street bridge and the US 3 bridge (1¹/₂ mi) on the left. After 2¹/₄ miles of meandering, pass under a railroad bridge, below which there is some turbulence. Garvin's Falls Dam (5 mi) comes quickly into sight. Portage on the left. There is a short Class II rapid below it.

In the next 5¹/₂ miles to the dam at Hooksett, pass the mouth of the Soucook River (5³/₄ mi) and the Suncook River (8³/₄ mi). About ¹/₄ mile above Hooksett Dam there are two nice boat-launching ramps on the left, but experienced paddlers who are carrying by hand can continue in low water as far as the abutment on the left (10¹/₂ mi). Carry past the parking area to another launching ramp below the dam.

There is some turbulence around the bridge abutments below the Hooksett Dam, then 7^1/$_4$ miles of smoothwater to Manchester. Amoskeag Bridge and the Manchester skyline can be seen from a long distance upstream. Take out at the bridge on the right to portage Amoskeag Dam. Look for concrete steps by the river and the Holiday Inn.

Manchester—Nashua   17^3/$_4$ mi

Description:	Flatwater, quickwater, Class II-III
Date checked:	1988, GE
Navigable:	Passable at most water levels
	Dam controlled, peak power generation
Scenery:	Forested, settled, urban
Maps:	USGS Manchester North, Manchester South,
	Nashua North

Gauge readings at Amoskeag Dam in Manchester can be obtained by calling the Public Service Company dispatcher (603-225-6182, x 2281). Flood stage is anything over 20,000 cubic feet per second. Spring runoff typically produces 12,000 to 15,000 cfs. Early summer levels run around 5,000 cfs, and dry summers bottom out at 1,200 to 1,300 cfs. At 5,000 to 12,000 cfs, the two most difficult rapids, Goffs Falls and Griffins Falls, are easy-to-moderate Class III; at high water, they wash out. The Merrimack moves a lot of water with a constant current of strong quickwater, rather than through rocky drops.

There is a mile of Class II rapids through Manchester. On the left bank the walls of old factories rise straight up from the river, and on the right there is a limited accesss highway. In high water, keep to the right.

Past two highway bridges and shortly below the rapids, the Piscataquog River (2 mi) enters on the right in South Manchester. A cascade of sewage, marked by a crowd of herring gulls, comes in on the left just above the Queen City Bridge, which is the third highway bridge below Amoskeag Dam. In 1^1/$_2$ miles there is a riffle, and soon the I-293 bridges comes into sight.

Land under the I-293 bridges ($4^{1}/_{4}$ mi) to scout the Class III drops, Griffins Falls and Goffs Falls, which can be run on either side but not in the middle. This spot can be reached on the right via a dirt road. In another $^{3}/_{4}$ mile there is a railroad bridge with a ledge starting just above it. It, too, can be run on either side, but not in the middle, where there is an island. This ledge can be inspected in advance from dirt roads on either side.

Below the railroad bridge (5 mi) there is smoothwater for $1^{1}/_{4}$ miles to a short Class II drop, and then more smoothwater for 2 miles to a longer Class II rapid just below a big power line. After 2-1/4 miles of smoothwater, the Souhegan River ($10^{1}/_{2}$ mi) enters on the right. Almost 3 miles downstream of the confluence with the Souhegan, on the right, are the best preserved remains of the old lock and canal system. In another mile there is a Class II rapid, followed by $3^{1}/_{4}$ miles of east paddling to the NH 111 bridge ($17^{3}/_{4}$ mi) in Nashua just below the mouth of the Nashua River on the right.

Nashua—Lowell   14 mi

Description:	Flatwater, quickwater
Date checked:	1988, GE
Navigable:	Passable at all water levels
Scenery:	Forested, settled, towns
Maps:	USGS Nashua South, Lowell

From the NH 111 bridge in Nashua, it is only 1 mile to the south end of town, where Salmon Brook enters on the right. The river is now all smoothwater. It passes between tilled fields and meadows for some distance, finally entering a section with wooded banks before it reaches the next bridge, MA 113, at Tyngsboro, Massachusetts, 5 miles below. There are more signs of human habitation in the next 4 miles to North Chelmsford, where Stony Brook enters on the right. In another 3 miles one arrives at Lowell. Take out at the public launching ramp above the dam.

The river is followed by the railroad. Watch for interesting old stone bridges and culverts spanning small tributaries.

Lowell Portage at Pawtucket Falls   1¹/₄ mi

Pawtucket Falls is not as canoeable as the people rescued from it seem to think.

Lowell—Lawrence   10¹/₂ mi

Description:	Flatwater, quickwater, Class I
Date checked:	1985
Navigable:	Passable at all water levels
Scenery:	Forested, towns, urban
Maps:	USGS Lowell, Lawrence
Portage:	(10¹/₂ mi L dam ¹/₄ mi)

The most convenient start below the dam is at the second bridge upstream on Beaver Brook. The river runs swiftly past factories, the mouth of the Concord River (1¹/₂ mi), and over the riffle at Hunts Falls (2 mi). During the remainder of the distance it gradually slows and passes under I-93 (8 mi) to Lawrence (10¹/₂ mi). Day-trippers should take out at any of the many canoe access points, while through-trippers should land on the left to carry the dam.

Lawrence—Newburyport   27³/₄ mi

Description:	Flatwater, quickwater, tidal
Date checked:	1985
Navigable:	Passable at all water levels, tidal
Scenery:	Forested, towns, urban
Maps:	USGS South Groveland, Ayers Village, Haverhill, Newburyport West and East

Put in at the ramp on the left behind the factories. The river has riffles for the first 3 miles, then becomes wide and smooth. After 1 mile the Spicket River enters on the left and the Shawsheen on the right. I-495 crosses at 1¹/₂, 5³/₄, and 7¹/₄ miles. In the bend to the north between the last bridges, the river becomes tidal. The last of four small bridges is Rock Village (16^1/$_4$ mi), with a picnic area on the right. The mouth of the Powwow is passed at 21 miles, and I-95 at 22 miles. Deer Island and several other islands lie in the river between this bridge and the US 1 bridge (24^3/$_4$ mi). The last 3 miles are wide and heavily used by large boats. Salisbury Beach Park is on the left and Plum Island on the right. Passing the breakwater is not recommended.

The tidal rise and fall at the Merrimack River entrance varies between 8^1/$_2$ and 9^1/$_2$ feet. High tide is about 5 minutes later than Boston and low tide 10 minutes later. At Newburyport, the respective differences increase to 15 minutes and 55 minutes, with corresponding increases farther up the river.

NASHUA RIVER   MA, NH

The Nashua River has two principal branches, the south, or main river, rising near Worcester, and the North Branch, formed by the junction of the Whitman and Nookagee rivers in West Fitchburg. The two branches meet at Lancaster Common and flow north to the Merrimack River at Nashua, New Hampshire. The main river is dammed at Clinton to form the Wachusett Reservoir, which supplies water to Boston. There is, therefore, usually little or no flow through the old riverbed between Clinton and the junction with the North Branch at Lancaster Common, so this branch has now become the principal headwater of the river.

The Nashua River has enjoyed a major rejuvenation since the time when the team assigned to check it for the previous guidebook refused to unload their canoe because of the pollution. Paddling the Nashua River is now an enjoyable experience and birds, wildlife, and fish are returning. For further information on the river contact the Nashua River Watershed Association (NRWA), 484 Main Street, Fitchburg, MA 01420. They print a river guidebook that locates the frequent access points and points of interest.

Leominster—Lancaster   10¹/₂ mi

Description:	**Quickwater,** Class I, **II**
Date checked:	1985
Navigable:	High water: spring
Scenery:	Forested, settled, towns
Maps:	USGS Fitchburg, Shirley, Clinton
Portages:	2 mi L dam
	6 mi L dam

Put in at the Searstown Mall. The paddling is easy through an open valley not far from the birthplace of Johnny Appleseed. The first dam is hard to see around a right-hand turn. Land on the left to carry. One Class II rapid is under a power line around a double island. The next dam is easier to spot and can be seen from Lunenburg Road. There is one last riffle before the MA 117 bridge, although the current continues, and curves and snags still trouble unskilled paddlers. The Lancaster Canoe Launch is at the Main Street Bridge.

Lancaster—Ayer   10¹/₂ mi

Description:	Quickwater
Date checked:	1985
Navigable:	Medium water
Scenery:	Forested, settled, towns
Maps:	USGS Clinton, Shirley, Ayer
Portage:	(10¹/₂ mi R dam)

Here the river sharply reverses itself and starts its northward swing. Below the confluence with the South Branch (¹/₂ mi) the river is much larger, with a strong current and fewer meanders. It passes under MA 117 (2 mi) by the mouth of the Still River on the right, and under MA 2 (8¹/₂ mi), and finally approaches the dam at the Ayer Ice Company.

Ayer—East Pepperell   **11 mi**

Description:	Flatwater, quickwater
Date checked:	1985
Navigable:	Passable at most water levels
Scenery:	Forested, towns
Maps:	USGS Ayer, Pepperell
Portages:	(11 mi R dam ¹/₂ mi)

Nonacoicus Brook enters on the left in 1 mile, and the Squannacook River enters on the left at 3 miles, just below the MA 2A bridge. It flows easily past MA 225 (5¹/₂ mi) and MA 119 (8¹/₄ mi), where it enters the extensive ponding from the next dam at East Pepperell. The Stony Wading Place was here before the bridge was built. The old dam remains are barely visible at low water. Ruins of the 1841 Oliver Howe paper mill are adjacent to the Groton Canoe Launch here on the right.

The Pepperell Pond is the most beautiful and interesting segment of the entire river. Although less than 3 miles in length as the crow flies, the maze of oxbows, backwaters, and meanders make it possible to spend an entire day here. A survey by a wildlife biologist hired by the NRWA confirmed that this area is unique in the diversity of its plant and animal life. Waterfowl and other birds are particularly abundant (flocks of forty to fifty great blue herons may be seen.) Conservation restriction and public land purchases will ensure that the Pepperell Pond will remain protected. The Nashua River has repeatedly been cited by the EPA and many other state, regional, and federal agencies for its remarkable progress. The growing NRWA greenway program has thus far protected over 45 of the 112 miles of the river bank; it is currently concentrating on the Pepperell Pond area.

The long portage is best made by car for ¹/₂ mile to the covered bridge on the Nashua River. Alternately, people continuing may put in at the Mill Street bridge on the Nissitissit River just to the North and run down the last mile of it to the Nashua.

East Pepperell—Mine Falls   9³/₄ mi

Description:	Flatwater, quickwater
Date checked:	1985
Navigable:	Passable at all water levels
Scenery:	Forested, settled, towns
Maps:	USGS Pepperell, Nashua South
Portages:	5¹/₄ mi e old dam at Ronnells Mills
	[9³/₄ mi R Mine Lot Falls (difficult) ¹/₄ mi]

On April 19, 1775, when the men of Pepperell had gone to Concord to answer the alarm, the women dressed in their husbands' clothing and armed themselves with whatever they could find. They patrolled the Mill Street bridge in East Pepperell and arrested a Tory, Captain Leonard Whiting of Hollis, who was bearing dispatches to the British in Boston.

From the put-in below the dam in East Pepperell it is only ³/₄ mile to the junction of the Nissitissit. The current is moderate as far as the broken dam at Ronnells Mills, just below the NH 111 bridge. Besides obvious problems, some spikes still protrude. This can be run, but only with scouting and good safety precaution.

The main flow of the river is on the right, which is free of debris from the old dam. At high water this is a short Class III run. There is convenient access on the right above, or the left below the dam.

From here to the first dam 1 mile west of Nashua the current slows. The take-out at Mine Lot Falls is a 700-foot carry, so one might be better advised to take out at the Horrigan Conservation Area off NH 111, about three-quarters of the way down.

Mine Lot Falls—Merrimack River 5¹/₂ mi

Description:	Flatwater, quickwater, possible rapids
Date checked:	1985
Navigable:	Passable at most water levels
Scenery:	Forested, settled, urban
Maps:	USGS Nashua South
Portages:	3³/₄ mi L dam (difficult footing) 200 yd along railroad track

Note: The dam is being rebuilt; the next two paragraphs may be obsolete.

Portage Mine Lot Falls on the right. This is the dam that forms the Nashua Canal, and the portage to the canal is easier than the one to the river.

The first rapids below the dam are sharp drops over sharp ledges—real boat eaters. Where the river separates around an island, they become easier. A good path leads high above the river, with a trail down to the river at almost the end of the rapids, about ¹/₄ mile.

Below the rapids the river wanders peacefully in a big loop to the left under the Everett Turnpike and a prize-winning pedestrian bridge.

Just before the last loop, a factory comes into sight on the right, with a solid line of factories around the next bend. Water from the canal exits under these factories. Below the stone-arch Main Street bridge is another dam that can be portaged on either side, although the right is shorter, and the bank is steep in either case.

The river is quickwater for the remaining 1³/₄ miles to the Merrimack. The chief obstruction is shopping carts.

Alternate Canal Trip 3 mi

Portage into the canal on the right (east) side of the Nashua River. The canal is sluggish and pleasant, passing under the same turnpike and pedestrian bridges as the river.

At the far end, the canal goes down the drain and emerges from underneath the factory. The canoeist can carry to the right down the railroad track and then straight ahead, bearing right to the Standard Hardware parking area by the river.

A more desirable carry is under a power line ¹/₂ mile upstream, where the river is only a short distance down the bank through the bushes.

River/Canal Circle Trip   about 6 mi

Put in the canal from the parking area behind the high school. There is also a convenient take-out for people coming downstream, better than at Mine Falls. Paddle left *upstream* toward the dam where a carry can be made with some effort over to the river. This is the best approach for anyone who wishes to run the rapids. Continue downstream to where the factory comes into view. There is a culvert on the right (the upstream end of the oxbow shown on the maps). Carry up to the canal and paddle back to the start.

SQUANNACOOK RIVER   MA

The Squannacook rises in Townsend and flows into the Nashua River in Ayer. It is a pretty stream with good current nearly all the way. Fallen trees may be a problem.

West Townsend—Nashua River   14³/₄

Description:	Flatwater, **quickwater,** Class I, II
Date checked:	1989, TA
Navigable:	High water
Scenery:	Forested, towns
Maps:	USGS Townsend, Shirley, Ayer
Portages:	2³/₄ mi R low dam
	6¹/₄ mi L dam
	10¹/₄ mi L Vose Mill
	11¹/₂ mi R dam

There are many possible runs on the Squannacook. For the upper, put in from a side road leading north from West Townsend (continuation of NH 123 to Mason) below a dam. A quarter mile downstream is a ledge, easily runnable. Just above Townsend at a right turn is Black Rock (1³/₄ mi), a huge boulder overhang. This area is public property (Howard Park).

Below the railroad trestle, within sight of the MA 119 bridge (2¹/₂ mi), there is a 4-foot dam, easily portaged on the right. About 200 yards below, an old dam at a blind left corner creates a wave. Below MA 13 a good current continues with beautiful hemlock-covered banks at many points. An old bridge abutment (4³/₄ mi), the access from Meetinghouse Road, marks the beginning of a swampy section that is not long, but difficult to get through. Below the swamp is the ponding from the dam at Townsend Harbor (6¹/₄ mi). At ordinary water levels it is possible, by lying flat in the canoe, to turn left above the dam and go through the sluiceway. Pass beyond the historic gristmill on the other side of the road. Take out there and slide the canoe down a narrow, steep path back into the river.

The river runs very swiftly on the left beside the mill, then gradually slows down. The river is larger and deeper than before. At a large pool, a picnic area is on the left. Stop on the left and scout the rapid below. This is a good take-out place for flatwater canoeists. To reach it take the road from the high school on MA 119 to West Groton. A large Department of Fisheries and Wildlife sign marks the dirt road to the river. This road is closed to vehicles, but a key may be obtained from the Northeast Wildlife District, Harris Street, Box 86, Acton, MA 01720.

A gauging station is at the first drop. Just around the corner to the left is another ledge, and below it is the third and most difficult drop, which has large waves. At a reading of 4 feet, the best route is middle for the first two drops and extreme left for the final one.

Boats can be carried where houses are seen on the left bank. Or carry up to the road at the water-supply building, which is reached by a paved road on the left above Vose Mill. Paddle into the big bay on the left, just above the mill.

Take out on the right to carry the dam ($10^1/4$ mi). Quickwater leads to another millpond. Do not go beneath the MA 225 bridge at West Groton; take out at the small clearing just to the right. From here, cross the road and carry down a short, steep slope to the put-in below the dam ($11^1/2$ mi).

Below West Groton the river regains its twisty, narrow character. A convenient take-out is about 1/4 mile upstream on the Nashua River at the MA 2A bridge.

NISSITISSIT RIVER   NH, MA

The Nissitissit rises in Lake Potanipo in Brookline, New Hampshire, and flows southeast into the Nashua River in Pepperell, Massachusetts. Although the entire river may be run in high water, the section from the source to the NH 13 crossing is not recommended.

This is a trout stream with clear water within 50 miles of Boston. Sharp turns, beaver dams, and fallen trees present the only difficulties.

Brookline—West Hollis $4^3/4$ mi

Description:	Quickwater, Class I
Date checked:	1989, TA
Navigable:	High water
Scenery:	Forested, rural
Map:	USGS Townsend

The first good put-in point is behind the fire station in Brookline. Take NH 13 north from Massachusetts and the first right after the Riverside Restaurant. If the water looks too low, put in 2 miles farther downstream at Bohannon's Bridge, which has a short Class II drop just above. From Bohannon's Bridge you will be out of sight of civilization for about $2^1/2$ miles, winding through Campbells Meadows.

There is a good take-out spot with parking on conservation land on the left bank at West Hollis. This spot is reached by taking Brookline Street from MA 111 just before it crosses the river in Pepperell.

West Hollis—Pepperell   3¹/₂ mi

Description:	Quickwater, Class I
Date checked:	1989, TA
Navigable:	High water
Scenery:	Forested
Map:	USGS Pepperell
Portages:	1¹/₄ mi e small dam
	3¹/₂ mi R dam in Pepperell

The 2 miles to the Prescott Street bridge constitute the most scenic part of the river. You can take out here up a steep bank to the road. After this point the stream is first quick and then shallow by the ruins of a colonial mill and then eventually quiet as you enter the mill pond. There is a carry of a few hundred feet to MA 111. Take out on the right.

Pepperell—Nashua River   1 mi

The rapids below the dam can be run. Most of them are Class II and end shortly below the MA 111 bridge. The Mill Street bridge (¹/₄ mi) is the last access before the Nashua river. From the confluence, it is another 4¹/₂ miles to the NH 111 bridge on the Nashua River.

BEAVER BROOK   NH, MA

Beaver Brook is a charming and pleasant, winding stream that flows from Beaver Lake in Derry to the Merrimack River at Lowell. There is a good current for most of that distance with some small beaver dams, some minor rapids, and occasional carries. The brook flows through several suburban communities. Increasingly, the settled areas intrude on the water, but portions of this brook offer near-wilderness.

Derry—West Windham   7 mi

Description:	Flatwater, quickwater
Date checked:	1988, RCG
Navigable:	High water: April
Scenery:	Forested, towns
Maps:	USGS Derry, Windham
Portages:	4 mi R dam at Kendall Pond 100 yd
	7 mi R dam at West Windham 40 yd

The original put-in on NH 28 is not recommended because of major sewer-pipe construction and numerous deadfalls along the river. An alternative put-in is off Gilcrest Road in Londonderry. In less than 1 mile, Beaver Brook enters Kendall Pond (3½ mi). Gilcrest Road can be reached by taking exit 4 off I-93 onto NH 102 toward Londonderry, and then taking the first left. Gilcrest crosses Beaver Brook just before intersecting with Kendall Pond Road.

One-half mile across the pond (4 mi) is the outlet, where there is a dam and a bridge. Take out on the right and carry across the road. Beware of snowmobile bridges just past the dam. For the next 3 miles the stream has logjams and beaver dams, and winds through meadows. Portage the dam at West Windham (7 mi) on the right. The NH 128 bridge is just below it.

West Windham—Second NH 128 bridge   3 mi

Description:	Quickwater, Class I
Date checked:	1989, JK
Navigable:	High water: March, April, wet fall
Scenery:	Forested
Map:	USGS Windham

The river bottom is gravelly, and numerous rocks give the canoeist practice in reading water, but the current is so slow. It is 1¾ miles to the NH 111 bridge, ¼ mile more to the next bridge, and then 1 mile to the second NH 128 bridge. In the last mile, there are two easy portages around a huge pine tree across the brook and an active and beaver dam.

Second NH 128 bridge—Collinsville   10¹/₂ mi

Description:	Flatwater, **quickwater,** Class II
Date checked:	1989, JK
Navigable:	High water: March, April, wet fall
Scenery:	Forested, towns
Maps:	USGS Windham, Lowell
Portages:	³/₄ mi L broken dam
	3³/₄ mi e small dam
	(10¹/₂ mi R dam in Collinsville)

This section of Beaver Brook is more demanding than the section above; it has a few rapids (many strainers in high water), and two interesting stone-arch bridges. Considerable new home construction near the water intrudes on the natural beauty of some sections, but near-wilderness prevails in others.

A house marks a left turn at a broken dam about ¹/₂ mile from the put-in. Take out on the left, and scout this dam before running it. Although the blocks are jagged, it can be run, lined, or portaged on the left. The second of two closely spaced bridges (Tallant Road) offers good access upstream on the left (1¹/₄ mi). Quickwater follows for 1¹/₂ miles to a bridge, now closed, and then for another mile to a small concrete dam (3³/₄ mi), which can be lifted over or run in the middle.

One-half mile past the second dam, a steel-beam bridge (4¹/₄ mi) on NH 111A must be carried at high water because of low clearance. It is ³/₄ mile to a stone-arch bridge and another ¹/₂ mile to the bridge on Old Bridge Street (5¹/₂ mi), opposite the shopping center on NH 38 in Pelham.

From the shopping center it is ³/₄ mile to the Willow Street bridge, and from there the brook winds for 4¹/₄ miles through meadows. There are some Class II rapids above the dam and bridge at Collinsville (10¹/₂ mi) in Dracut. Take out 150 yards above the dam, on the right, at a grassy launching area.

Collinsville—Merrimack River   3¹/₂ mi

Description:	Flatwater, quickwater, Class II
Date checked:	1989, JK
Navigable:	Passable at most water levels: rapids require medium water
Scenery:	Forested, towns
Portages:	2¹/₂ mi R dam 50 yd
	3 mi L dam 400 yd

People continuing downstream should land on the left to portage the dam. Although the water quality and trash detract somewhat, this is still a worthwhile paddle.

Class II rapids run below the dam for ¹/₄ mile, with a couple of small ledges that are exciting at high water. The river then resumes its small, meandering character, passing under farm bridges at 1 and 1¹/₄ miles. The next bridge (2¹/₄ mi) offers good access. Around the corner and within sight of Parker Avenue is a 10-foot dam.

The next dam is confined entirely between two factories. Take out at a Dracut municipal structure on the left, 200 yards above the dam, where the ponding brook narrows again. Access is difficult below the dam, and it is only ¹/₂ mile to Martin Street, which is a recommended put-in for the Merrimack River below Pawtucket Falls.

CONCORD RIVER   MA

The Concord is formed by the confluence of the Assabet and Sudbury Rivers in Concord. The water in the Concord and its tributaries has, at various times, been used to power mills and factories, flood the Middlesex Canal, and supply water to Boston. Now, some of the dams have been washed out, the canal is dry, and Boston relies primarily upon the Quabbin Reservoir for water. Most of the Sudbury and all of the Concord above North Billerica are influenced by the dam at Talcott Mills. The Concord has wide, marshy flood plains, many of which are included in the Great Meadows National Wildlife Refuge. The meadow makes travel against the wind difficult.

Concord—North Billerica   10³/₄ mi

Description:	Flatwater
Date checked:	1989, JM
Navigable:	Passable at all water levels
Scenery:	Forested, rural, settled
Maps:	USGS Concord, Billerica
Portages:	(10³/₄ mi R dam at Talbot Mills—difficult in high water)

From the Lowell Road bridge in Concord, 200 yards below the confluence of the Assabet and Sudbury rivers, the Concord flows northeast. The river passes under the Old North Bridge replica. This area is a part of the Minute Man National Historical Park. The river flows northeast for 2 miles and then swings north, keeping Balls Hill on the left. In another 2 miles the MA 225 bridge (4³/₄ mi) is reached. The river continues past the MA 4 bridge (6¹/₂ mi), the US 3 bridge (7³/₄ mi), the MA 3A bridge (9³/₄ mi), and the North Billerica bridge (10¹/₄ mi) to the dam at Talbot Mills (10³/₄ mi).

If you are continuing on to the Merrimack, the portage around this dam is difficult. There is no easy entry into the water below the dam due to industrial fencing. It is best to scout this area before arriving at the dam. In low water, the dam may be portaged over the edge of the dam on the right.

North Billerica—Lowell   4¹/₂ mi

Description:	Flatwater, Class II
Date checked:	1989, JM
Navigable:	Passable at most water levels
Scenery:	Urban
Maps:	USGS Billerica, Lowell
Portages:	3 mi e 10 ft dam —difficult
	(4¹/₄ mi R 20 ft dam—difficult)

Passage around the three dams is difficult, but this section provides year-round whitewater. The first 3 miles are flatwater to the first dam. The portage is difficult. Rapids continue for $^3/_4$ mile down a steep-sided valley past factories. Below the next bridge keep right, at an island. This section should be scouted from the right bank. Where it breaks out of the gorge, the rapids culminate in a ledge that has a Class III+ hole. The next $^3/_4$ mile has two stretches of whitewater with a difficult drop over a ledge.

ASSABET RIVER   MA

The Assabet River rises in Westboro and flows northeastward to Concord, where its confluence with the Sudbury creates the Concord River. Although many dams have eliminated most of the rapids, there are still a number of short, fairly attractive trips that can be made.

Westboro—Hudson   11$^1/_4$ mi

Description:	**Flatwater,** quickwater, Class I
Date checked:	1985
Navigable:	High and medium water: March, April
Scenery:	Forested, rural, towns
Maps:	USGS Shrewsbury, Marlboro, Hudson
Portages:	3$^3/_4$ mi R dam at Northboro 10 yd
	4$^3/_4$ mi R dam at Woodside 15 yd
	(11$^1/_4$ mi L dam at Hudson—difficult 200 yd)

In its upper stretches the Assabet is still a small stream. Most of this portion is runnable all year, but shallow places below the dam in Northboro and through Chapinville make the spring preferable. The scenery includes frequent views of marshes and farms, with only a few interruptions from road crossings and dams.

From the put-in at the MA 9 bridge, there are 3$^3/_4$ miles of winding, marshy river to the dam in Northboro. This dam, the site of a gristmill around 1700, should be portaged on the right. If the water is high enough, the riffles under the US 20 bridge just below can be run; otherwise carry around the bridge. Riffles continue below this bridge under an old mill. This mill draws its power from a dam on Cold Harbor Brook, which enters from the left, the main river is clear of obstructions. Just below, the river widens into a pond above the dam at Woodside. Just above are a high stone aqueduct bridge and a low bridge on a side road. Portage the dam itself (4³/4 mi), and the low bridge if necessary, on the right. Riffles continue below, as the river runs navigably under another mill and between stone walls.

For the next 6¹/2 miles the banks alternate between marsh and farmland. The river is occasionally overhung and obstructed. A number of small bridges are passed, including those of I-495. The portage around the dam in Hudson (11¹/4 mi) is complicated by fences and concrete retaining walls. Carry on the left side through gas stations to a put-in just below the MA 85 bridge.

Hudson—Maynard   8¹/2 mi

Description:	Flatwater, quickwater, Class I
Date checked:	1989, GE
Navigable:	Passable at all water levels
Scenery:	Forested, marshy, towns
Maps:	USGS Hudson, Maynard
Portages:	3¹/3 mi L dam at Gleasondale 100 yd
	5¹/2 mi (lift over Barton Rd into Boons Pond—optional)
	(8¹/2 mi L first dam at Maynard 15 yd)

Water quality between Hudson and Maynard has improved over the past ten years. Put in along a dirt road paralleling the river's south bank between Broad Street and Forest Street in Hudson, ¹/2 mile east of the MA 85 bridge. Quickwater is found for the first mile under Forest Street and past old factories, cemeteries, and rail beds to the Main Street bridge (1 mi). The Cox Street Bridge is passed at 1¹/4 miles. Duckweed mats are often found in this area, or down by Boons Pond.

Below Cox Street the Assabet enters marshland. The river widens and curves around a large farm on the right. Gleasondale Dam (3¹/2 mi) follows. Portage left along a lightly worn path to a road. Turn

right on the road, cross the river, and slide the boats down a short
steep bank on the right, just after crossing the bridge. This portage
passes through private property; consideration and courtesy is urged.
The shallow rapids below may have to be walked in low water, then
the MA 62 bridge (3^1/$_2$ mi) is passed.

In another mile the Assabet splits around an island and widens as
a round-roofed structure resembling an airplane hangar appears on
the right. This marks the approach to Boons Pond outlet on the right
(5^1/$_2$ mi). For a delightful picnic spot and side trip, Boons Pond may
be reached by paddling 70 yards of shallow, marshy outlet and
portaging (10 yd) Barton Road. A sandy beach is found 800 yards
due east, directly across the pond. Cars may be parked near the beach
as an alternate take-out.

The Assabet continues past the outlet and turns sharply left,
narrowing between stone embankments of an old railroad bridge.
After a few more turns, Boon Road bridge (6 mi) is passed, and the
river makes a wide straight path for Maynard. A golf course appears
on the left before reaching the Tuttle Hill bridge with good access
(8^1/$_4$ mi). The dam above Maynard (8^1/$_2$ mi) should be portaged on
the left.

Maynard—Concord   8^1/$_2$ mi

Description:	**Flatwater,** quickwater, Class I-II
Date checked:	1987, GE
Navigable:	High or medium water: March through May
	Low water: rapids in Maynard impassable
Scenery:	Forested, settled
Maps:	USGS Maynard, Concord
Portages:	2^1/$_4$ mi L second dam in Maynard 50 yd

The rapids in Maynard provide good training for novice
whitewater boaters. The remainder of the run is smooth and runnable
all year. The pollution of the water, however, is less offensive when
the water level is up.

Put in on the right bank from a dirt road next to the Pace Company. There are 1¹/₂ miles of easy Class II rapids through Maynard. These can be malodorous and impassable in low water. Below the MA 27/62 bridge in Maynard Center, the rapids end, followed by ³/₄ mile of flatwater to the second Maynard dam (2¹/₄ mi). Portage on the left.

Below Maynard, swift current and two quick crossings of MA 62 give way to another flatwater section above the broken dam in West Concord (4 mi). The gatehouse has been washed out, so that the dam is runnable on the far right. **Caution!** Scout for obstructions. The next 2 miles contain a mixture of slow and moderate current, and highway and railroad bridges. After the Concord Reformatory and the MA 2 bridge (6 mi), the river has high banks on the left and meadows on the right.

Spencer Brook, which enters on the left 1¹/₄ miles below MA 2, was often spoken of by Thoreau. This brook can be ascended a short distance, but tall marsh grasses overhang the canoe, and the abrupt turns make passage difficult. **Caution!** Just past Spencer Brook there is a large rock in mid-river called Gibraltar, and there are several other rocks that must be avoided. The river then makes two graceful curves with wooded banks. A short distance above the junction with the Sudbury River is the site of the hemlocks made famous by Hawthorne in *Mosses from an Old Manse*. These were on the right bank at the foot of Nashawtuc Hill, but they are now largely replaced by willows. The next take-out is 200 yards down the Concord River at the Lowell Street bridge (8¹/₂ mi).

ASSABET BROOK   MA

This tributary of the Assabet River provides a short, pleasant run on a narrow stream. The water is moderately clean in contrast to the main river, which is darker and dirtier. There are a number of obstructions necessitating short portages.

Stow—Maynard   4¹/₂ mi

Description:	Lakes, **quickwater,** Class I
Date checked:	1985
Navigable:	High or medium water: April through July
	Low water: rapids in Maynard impassable
Scenery:	Forested
Maps:	USGS Hudson, Maynard
Portages:	1¹/₄ mi R dam on Wheeler Pond 20 yd
	2 mi R dam on Fletcher Pond 20 yd

Put in at the MA 117 bridge about a mile west of Stow. The stream, with a good current at this point, splits immediately around an island. The woods give way to marshier banks, and the Stow Country Club is passed on the right. The brook leads into ¹/₂-mile-long Wheeler Pond. Portage the outlet dam (1¹/₄ mi) on the right, and, if necessary because of low clearance, the stone bridge on Wheeler Road just below. Another marshy ¹/₂-mile brings the paddler to the MA 62 bridge, shortly below which Fletcher Pond is entered. After the portage at this outlet dam (2 mi), there are 1³/₄ miles of river with good current and occasional riffles. Watch out for culverts. The brook passes the Assabet Country Club—with another low bridge—just before joining the Assabet River (3³/₄ mi). A take-out is possible at the bridge ¹/₄ mile down the Assabet or at the dam (4¹/₂ mi) just above the MA 117 bridge in Maynard.

SUDBURY RIVER   MA

The Sudbury joins the Assabet in Concord to form the Concord River. Canoeing above Framingham Center is impractical due to the size of the stream and reservoir-use restrictions. There is generally enough water below Framingam, however, to float a canoe despite the reservoirs.

Framingham Center—Concord   **20¹/₄ mi**

Description:	Lake, **flatwater,** quickwater
Date checked:	1989, JM
Navigable:	Passable at most water levels
Scenery:	Settled, forested
Maps:	USGS Framingham, Natick, Maynard, Concord
Portages:	2 mi e low dam 10 yd
	3¹/₂ mi R dam at Saxonville

The best put-in is at a parking lot off Union Avenue, behind a sandwich shop, northwest of the bridge, and just south of MA 9. The river is broad and sluggish, with many bridges. Two miles below the put-in there is a low but dangerous dam, which is easily portaged. The next mile to Saxonville is more pond-like. Portage the Saxonville Dam (3¹/₂ mi) on the right, where there is a good access point.

Saxonville is soon left behind. High, wooded banks give way to wide meadows. From Saxonville to North Billerica on the Concord there are 27¹/₂ miles of unobstructed flatwater. Saxonville can be reached by taking Edgell Road, the right fork off Central Street, north from MA 9 in Framingham Center.

There is ¹/₄-mile of quickwater between steep embankments below the dam. The river turns left and passes under the Danforth Street bridge (4¹/₄ mi—good access) and another bridge. The remains of a stone bridge built in 1673 are passed at 6 miles. There are four more bridges before the MA 117 bridge (15¹/₂ mi), which is ¹/₂ mile before the river enters Fairhaven Bay. This is Great Meadows.

Fairhaven Bay (16 mi) is a ¹/₂-mile-long lake on the border between Concord and Lincoln. The river is wider as it leaves the bay. Just below a railroad bridge is the Old South Bridge (19¹/₄ mi), originally built around 1660. Canoe rentals are available at the South Bridge Boat House. After passing the site of an old railroad bridge (20 mi), the Assabet joins the Sudbury to form the Concord. The next take-out is 200 yards down the Concord River at the Lowell Street bridge (20¹/₄ mi).

SPICKET RIVER   NH, MA

The Spicket River rises in Island Pond in Hampstead and flows south to reach the Merrimack at Lawrence. The upper and lower parts are not practical to paddle, but the middle section offers a more pleasant quickwater run than might be expected in such a settled area.

Town Farm Road—Methuen, MA   8 mi

Description:	Quickwater
Date checked:	1988, RD
Navigable:	High water: March and April or after rain
Scenery:	Wooded, settled
Maps:	USGS Ayers Village, Lawrence

A start can be made at Town Farm Road, just below an alder swamp, or at NH 97, 1 mile south. The brook is small, and it wriggles back and forth among the trees, sometimes up to the backyards of houses. The least attractive section is near the trash from the shopping center along NH 28 (5 mi). After another mile the new river channel parallels I-93, with access to the old channel through a culvert. The river passes under the interstate ramp (7 mi) and under a railroad bridge. Take out—with permission—on the left above the highway bridge.

Below here are two dams, close together, and the river runs over at least two more dams, one of which is confined between factory walls. The Merrimack is 4 miles below.

SHAWSHEEN RIVER   MA

The Shawsheen rises in Bedford and flows northeast into the Merrimack at Lawrence. The section above Ballardville is recommended as one of the better paddles close to Boston. All but the uppermost part of the river (MA 4 to US 3) can be run through the spring in most years. The section below Ballardville is not recommended due to dams, factories, and pollution. Further information can be obtained from the Shawsheen Watershed Association, 121 Pond Street, Tewksbury, MA 01876.

Bedford—Ballardville 15¼ mi

Description:	**Flatwater,** quickwater, Class I
Date checked:	1988, GE
Navigable:	High water: April
	Medium water: May and June
Scenery:	Forested, settled
Maps:	USGS Concord, Billerica, Wilmington, Lawrence
Portages:	1+ mi R rapids below MA 62 bridge (rough) 250 yd
	(15¼ mi R dam)

In high water, put in at the Great Road Shopping Center at MA 4/225 in Bedford. The stream is small and somewhat obstructed by branches until the Page Road bridge. The rapids below the MA 62 bridge must be carried on the right in low water. The river then becomes slow and meandering past the US 3 bridge (2 mi) to the Middlesex Turnpike (3 mi). Quickwater leads to the MA 3A bridge (4½ mi), where the low bridge may require a portage right. The Shawsheen flows for the next 3¼ miles to the MA 129 bridge through wooded or marshy banks. There is a gauge on river right at the bridge. 2½ is low but runnable. There is a minor rapid below the bridge past the ruins of the Middlesex Canal viaduct (7¾ mi). Land on the left past the ruins to see the historic marker here. In the next mile, pass a railroad bridge, the low Whipple Road bridge, and the mouth of Content Brook.

The MA 38 bridge is a convenient place to launch or take out (10 mi). There are some minor rapids and fast current in the next 2 miles, past a triple-barreled culvert on a minor road. The river then meanders again and passes under I-93 (no access), followed by 2 miles of marshy flowage to the dam at Ballardville. Take out right above the dam.

Ballardville Dam—Merrimack River   8¹/₄ mi

Description:	Flatwater, quickwater
Date checked:	1988, GE
Navigable:	Medium water: May and June
Scenery:	Forested, marsh, settled, urban
Portages:	2³/₄ mi R broken dam (beware water entering R below dam)
	3¹/₄ mi R dam 200 yd
	4³/₄ mi e roll dam—dangerous

Carry around the left side of the building to the parking lot. Put in below the unrunnable dam, where the Shawsheen is a narrow channel. It soon opens up and, in ¹/₄ mile, makes a sharp turn into a heavily wooded area. The stream entering left is the remains of the old river channel. The stream from Pomps Pond enters right.

The woods begin to thin out and houses appear as the channel enters a meadow area. The channel turns left between two stone pillars. Good access is available right on Center Street (2 mi). Quickwater flows under a stone-arch railroad bridge in this area. The remains of the next dam (2³/₄ mi) can be run after scouting, or portage right. A hanging pipe at the Essex Street bridge (3 mi) may cause trouble in high water.

After a sharp left turn take out right, just downstream of a brick blockhouse, to portage the 12-foot Stevens Street dam. Below Main Street (3¹/₂ mi) banks are earthen a short distance then return to stone walls; Balmoral Street bridge is a stone arch. The roll dam at the American Wool Company must be run, as portaging is impractical.

Caution! Two hundred yards below MA 133 (4¹/₂ mi), two iron pipes cross: take out and portage the dangerous roll dam below, site of several drownings.

The Shawsheen soon comes to an I-495 ramp and a stone-arch railroad bridge, then enters a wooded section with many downed trees. Below MA 114 (5³/₄ mi), the river enters a swamp and passes a broken stone bridge. A triple culvert leads under I-495 (7 mi). After ¹/₄ mile, where the river turns away from I-495, a 100-foot portage cuts off a long oxbow often blocked by fallen trees. After the Massachusetts Avenue bridge (7³/₄ mi), the river wanders along I-495, eventually flowing through another triple culvert, 300 yards long and very dark, into the Merrimack River. Just downstream is the I-495 bridge and several good places to take out on the right.

LITTLE RIVER   NH, MA

Map:	USGS Haverhill

This stream is runnable from Plaistow, New Hampshire, to within a mile of the Merrimack River in Haverhill, Massachusetts, at which point it runs into a culvert. It is a small quickwater stream that is canoeable only at high water.

Begin the run from Main Street in Plaistow (NH 121A) just east of NH 125. In ¹/₂ mile the stream passes beneath Westville Road, and within another ¹/₂ mile beneath two bridges, the second of which is NH 125. It passes under NH 121 (1¹/₂ mi) just above the state line. The stream remains small until it passes under I-495 (3 mi) and enters the backwater of a dam in Haverhill. Much of this flowage is paralleled by railroad tracks. The best take-out points in Haverhill are at a playground (5 mi) on the right 150 yards past a railroad bridge and ¹/₂ mile above the dam, or at Benjamin and Apple streets just above the dam.

POWWOW RIVER   NH, MA

This small stream in southeastern New Hampshire has two sections that offer pleasant canoeing in largely isolated areas.

Kingston—Powwow Pond   **4 mi**

Description:	Pond, flatwater, quickwater
Date checked:	1985
Navigable:	High water: stream
Scenery:	Marsh, forested
Maps:	USGS Haverhill 15, Exeter
Portage:	(4 mi dam and rocky stream 2 mi)

The first section begins in Kingston, New Hampshire. Put in just below the outlet of Great Pond where NH 111 and NH 125 cross the river. One-and-a-half miles of narrow stream in a picturesque marsh give way to 1¼ miles of more open water above Powwow Pond, where there are many cottages. Take out at the east end of the pond to the left of a railroad bridge (4 mi). A short dirt road leads out to NH 107A.

Portage by car 2 miles via MA 107A to Chase Road. Put in from the dirt road on the left just before the river.

Chase Road—Tuxbury Pond   **4¹/₂ mi**

Description:	Pond, flatwater, quickwater
Date checked:	1985
Navigable:	Medium water
Scenery:	Marsh, forested
Map:	USGS Newburyport West

From Chase Road there are 2¹/₂ miles of narrow stream through thick woods, then another mile of more open stream below the first bridge. It is a mile across the pond to the dam at the outlet, just across the state line in Amesbury, Massachusetts.

Lake Gardner—Merrimack River   2¹/₄ mi

Description:	Flatwater, tidal
Navigable:	Navigable except in low water
Scenery:	Urban, settled
Map:	USGS Newburyport West
Portages:	0 mi R Lake Gardner dam 20 yd
	¹/₂ mi R small dam, falls below 500 yd

Carry over the earthen part of the dam. Within the next ³/₄ mile there are three low bridges, a small broken dam (to be rebuilt), an unrunnable falls, and a tunnel through town. Take out below the third bridge and above the footbridge to avoid the hidden falls below. Carry across busy Market Street, then down Mill Street opposite an impressive old mill.

For the next 1¹/₂ miles, plan to go with the outgoing tide. Industrial shores soon give way to woods and marsh. In 1 mile are the NH 110 and I-495 bridges. In another ¹/₂ mile, just below the Main Street bridge, is the Merrimack. Go right, around the large marina, and up the Merrimack 100 yards to the town ramp to take out. If swift currents make this impossible, take out at the steep-banked Alliance Park, on the left at the confluence.

APPENDIX

Safety Code of the American Whitewater Affiliation

The following code, adopted in 1959 and revised in 1987, is reprinted with the permission of the American Whitewater Affiliation, 146 N. Brockton, Palatine, IL 60067.

I. PERSONAL PREPAREDNESS AND RESPONSIBILITY

1. **Be a competent swimmer,** with the ability to handle yourself underwater.

2. **Wear a life jacket.** A snug fitting, vest-type life preserver offers back and shoulder protection as well as the flotation needed to swim safely in whitewater.

3. **Wear a solid, correctly fitting helmet** when upsets are likely. This is essential in kayaks or covered canoes, and recommended for open canoeists using thigh straps and rafters running steep drops.

4. **Do not boat out of control.** Your skills should be sufficient to stop or reach shore before reaching danger. Do not enter a rapid unless you are reasonably sure that you can run it safely or swim it without injury.

5. **Whitewater rivers contain many hazards which are not always easily recognized. The following are the most frequent killers:**

    A. **HIGH WATER.** The river's speed and power increase tremendously as the flow increases, raising the difficulty of most rapids. Rescue becomes progressively harder as the water rises, adding to the danger. Floating debris and strainers make even an easy rapid quite hazardous. It is often misleading to judge the river level at the put in, since a small rise in a wide, shallow place will be multiplied many times where the water narrows. Use reliable gauge information whenever possible, and be aware that sun on snowpack, hard rain, and upstream releases may greatly increase the flow.

B. COLD. Cold drains your strength, and robs you of the ability to make sound decisions on matters affecting your survival. Cold water immersion, because of the initial shock and the rapid heat loss which follows, is especially dangerous. Dress appropriately for bad weather or sudden immersion in the water. When the water temperature is less than 50 degrees F, a wetsuit or drysuit is essential for protection if you swim. Next best is wool or pile clothing under a waterproof shell. In this case, you should also carry waterproof matches and a change of clothing in a waterproof bag. If, after prolonged exposure, a person experiences uncontrollable shaking, loss of coordination, or difficulty speaking, he or she is hypothermic and needs your assistance.

C. STRAINERS. Brush, fallen trees, bridge pilings, undercut rocks or anything else which allows river currents to sweep through can pin boats and boaters against the obstacle. Water pressure on anything trapped this way can be overwhelming. Rescue is often extremely difficult. Pinning may occur in fast current, with little or no whitewater to warn of the danger.

D. DAMS, WEIRS, LEDGES, REVERSALS, HOLES AND HYDRAULICS. When water drops over an obstacle, it curls back on itself, forming a strong upstream current which may be capable of holding a boat or a swimmer. Some holes make for excellent sport; others are proven killers. Paddlers who cannot recognize the differences should avoid all but the smallest holes. Hydraulics around man-made dams must be treated with utmost respect regardless of their height or the level of the river. Despite their seemingly benign appearance, they can create an almost escape-proof trap. The swimmer's only exit from the "drowning machine" is to dive below the surface when the downstream current is flowing beneath the reversal.

E. BROACHING. When a boat is pushed against a rock by a strong current, it may collapse and wrap. This is especially dangerous to kayak and decked canoe paddlers; these boats will collapse and the combination of indestructible hulls and tight outfitting may create a deadly trap. Even without entrapment, releasing pinned boats can be extremely time-consuming and dangerous. To avoid pinning, throw your weight downstream towards the rock. This allows the current to slide harmlessly underneath the hull.

6. **Boating alone is discouraged.** The minimum party is three people or two craft.

7. **Have a frank knowledge of your boating ability,** and don't attempt rivers or rapids which lie beyond that ability.

   A. Develop the paddling skills and teamwork required to match the river you plan to boat. Most good paddlers develop skills gradually, and attempts to advance too quickly will compromise your safety and equipment.

   B. Be in good physical and mental condition, consistent with the difficulties which may be expected. Make adjustments for loss of skills due to age, health, fitness. Any health limitations must be explained to your fellow paddlers prior to starting the trip.

8. **Be practiced in self-rescue,** including escape from an overturned craft. The Eskimo roll is strongly recommended for decked boaters who run rapids of Class IV or greater, or who paddle in cold environmental conditions.

9. **Be trained in rescue skills,** CPR, and first aid with special emphasis on the recognizing and treating of hypothermia. It may save your friend's life.

10. **Carry equipment needed for unexpected emergencies,** including footwear which will protect your feet when walking out, a throw rope, knife, whistle and waterproof matches. If you wear eyeglasses, tie them on and carry a spare pair on long trips. Bring cloth repair tape on short runs, and a full repair kit on isolated rivers. Do not wear bulky jackets, ponchos, heavy boots, or anything else which could reduce your ability to survive a swim.

11. Despite the mutually supportive group structure described in this code, individual paddlers are ultimately responsible for their own safety, and must assume sole responsibility for the following decisions:

    A. The decision to participate on any trip. This includes an evaluation of the expected difficulty of the rapids under the conditions existing at the time of the put in.

    B. The selection of appropriate equipment, including a boat design suited to their skills and the appropriate rescue and survival gear.

    C. The decision to scout any rapid, and to run or portage according to their best judgement. Other members of the group may offer advice, but paddlers should resist pressure from anyone to paddle beyond their skills. It is also their responsibility to decide whether to pass up any walk-out or take-out opportunity.

    D. All trip participants should constantly evaluate their own and their group's safety, voicing their concerns and following what they believe to be the best course of action. Paddlers are encouraged to speak with anyone whose actions on the water are dangerous, whether they are part of your group or not.

II. BOAT AND EQUIPMENT PREPAREDNESS

1. Test new and different equipment under familiar conditions before relying on it for difficult runs. This is especially true when adopting a new boat design or outfitting system. Low-volume craft may present additional hazards to inexperienced or poorly conditioned paddlers.

2. Be sure your boat and gear are in good repair before starting a trip. The more isolated and difficult the run, the more rigorous the inspection should be.

3. Install flotation bags in non-inflatable craft, securely fixed in each end, designed to displace as much water as possible. Inflatable boats should have multiple air chambers and be test inflated before launching.

4. Have strong, properly sized paddles or oars for controlling your craft. Carry sufficient spares for the length and difficulty of the trip.

5. Outfit your boat safely. The ability to exit your boat quickly is an essential component of safety in rapids. It is your responsibility to see that there is absolutely nothing to cause entrapment when coming free of an upset craft. This includes:

A. Spray covers which won't release reliably or which release prematurely.

B. Boat outfitting too tight to allow a fast exit, especially in low-volume kayaks or decked canoes. This includes low-hung thwarts in canoes lacking adequate clearance for your feet and kayak footbraces which fail or allow your feet to become wedged under them.

C. Inadequately supported decks which collapse on a paddler's legs when a decked boat is pinned by water pressure. Inadequate clearance with the deck because of your feet or build.

D. Loose ropes which cause entanglement. Beware of any length of loose line attached to a whitewater boat. All items must be tied tightly and excess line eliminated; painters, throw lines, and safety rope systems must be completely and effectively stored. Do not knot the end of a rope, as it can get caught in cracks between rocks.

6. Provide ropes which permit you to hold on to your craft so it may be rescued. The following methods are recommended.

A. Kayaks and covered canoes should have grab loops of ¼″ + rope or equivalent webbing sized to admit a normal-sized hand. Stern painters are permissible if properly secured.

B. Open canoes should have secured anchored bow and stern painters consisting of 8–10 feet of ¼″ + line. These must be secured in such a way that they are readily accessible, but cannot come loose accidentally. Grab loops are acceptable, but are more difficult to reach after an upset.

C. Rafts and dories may have taut perimeter lines threaded through the loops provided. Footholds should be designed so that a paddler's feet cannot be forced through them, causing entrapment. Flip lines should be carefully and reliably stowed.

7. Know your craft's carrying capacity, and how added loads affect boat handling in whitewater. Most rafts have a minimum crew size which can be added to on day trips or in easy rapids. Carrying more than two paddlers in an open canoe when running rapids is not recommended.

8. Car top racks must be strong and attach positively to the vehicle. Lash your boat to each crossbar, then tie the ends of the boats directly to the bumpers for added security. This arrangement should survive all but the most violent accident.

III. GROUP PREPAREDNESS AND RESPONSIBILITY

1. Organizations. River trips should be regarded as common adventures by all participants, except on specially designated instructional or guided trips. The group is collectively responsible for the conduct of the trip, and participants are individually responsible for judging their own capabilities and for their own safety as the trip progresses.

2. River Conditions. The group should have a reasonable knowledge of the difficulty of the run. Participants should evaluate this information and adjust their plans accordingly. If the run is exploratory or no one is familiar with the river, maps and guidebooks, if available, should be examined. The group should secure accurate flow information; the more difficult the run, the more important this will be. Be aware of possible changes in river level and how this will affect the difficulty of the run. If the trip involves tidal stretches, secure appropriate information on tides.

3. Group equipment should be suited to the difficulty of the river. The group should always have a throw line available, and one line per boat is recommended on difficult runs. The list may include: carabiners, prussick loops, first aid kit, flashlight, folding saw, fire starter, guidebooks, maps, food, extra clothing, and any other rescue or survival items suggested by conditions. Each item is not required on every run, and this list is not meant to be a substitute for good judgement.

4. **Keep the group compact,** but maintain sufficient spacing to avoid collisions. If the group is large, consider dividing into smaller groups or using the buddy system as an additional safe-guard. Space yourselves closely enough to permit good communication, but not so close as to interfere with one another in rapids.

   A. **The lead paddler** sets the pace. When in front, do not get in over your head. Never run drops when you cannot see a clear route to the bottom or, for advanced paddlers, a sure route to the next eddy. When in doubt, stop and scout.

   B. **Keep track** of all group members. Each boat keeps the one behind it in sight, stopping if necessary. Know how many people are in your group and take head counts regularly. No one should paddle ahead or walk out without first informing the group. Weak paddlers should stay at the center of a group, and not allow themselves to lag behind. If the group is large and contains a wide range of abilities, a designated "sweep boat" should bring up the rear.

   C. **Courtesy.** On heavily used rivers, do not cut in front of a boater running a drop. Always look upstream before leaving eddies to run or play. Never enter a crowded drop or eddy when no room for you exists. Passing other groups in a rapid may be hazardous: it's often safer to wait upstream until the group ahead has passed.

5. **Float Plan.** If the trip is into a wilderness area or for an extended period of time, plans should be filed with a responsible person who will contact the authorities if you are overdue. It may be wise to establish checkpoints along the way where civilization could be contacted if necessary. Knowing the location of possible help and preplanning escape routes can speed rescue.

6. **Drugs.** The use of alcohol or mind-altering drugs before or during river trips is not recommended. It dulls reflexes, reduces de-

cision making ability, and may interfere with important survival reflexes.

7. **Instruction or guided trips.** In this format, a person assumes the responsibilities of a trip leader. He or she may pass judgement on a participant's qualifications, check equipment, and assume responsibilities for the conduct of the trip normally taken by the group as a whole.

   A. These trips must be clearly designated as such in advance, as they could expose the leader to legal liability. Trip or personal liability insurance should be considered.

   B. Even on trips with a designated leader, participants must recognize that whitewater rivers have inherent hazards, that each person is still responsible for their decision to participate and their safety on the water.

IV. GUIDELINES FOR RIVER RESCUE

1. **Recover from an upset with an Eskimo roll** whenever possible. Evacuate your boat immediately if there is imminent danger of being trapped against rocks, brush, or any other kind of strainer.

2. **If you swim, hold on to your boat.** It has much flotation and is easy for rescuers to spot. Get to the upstream end so that you cannot be crushed between a rock and your boat by the force of the current. Persons with good balance may be able to climb on top of a swamped boat or flipped kayak and paddle to shore.

3. **Release your craft if this will improve your chances,** especially if the water is cold or dangerous rapids lie ahead. Actively attempt self-rescue whenever possible by swimming for safety. Be prepared to assist others who may come to your aid.

   A. **When swimming in shallow or obstructed rapids,** lie on your back **with feet held high** and pointed downstream. Do not attempt to stand in fast-moving water; if your foot wedges on the bottom, fast water will push you under and keep you there. Get to slow or very shallow water before attempting to stand or walk. Look ahead! Avoid possible pinning situations including undercut rocks, strainers, downed trees, holes, and other dangers by swimming away from them.

B. If the rapids are deep and powerful, roll over onto your stomach and swim aggressively for shore. Watch for eddies and slackwater and use them to get out of the current. Strong swimmers can effect a powerful upstream ferry and get to shore fast. If the shores are obstructed with strainers or undercut rocks, however, it is safer to "ride the rapid out" until a safer escape can be found.

4. **If others spill and swim, go after the boaters first.** Rescue boats and equipment only if this can be done safely. While participants usually assist one another to the best of their ability, they should do so only if they can, in their judgement, do so safely. The first duty of a rescuer is not to compound the problem by becoming another victim.

5. **The use of rescue lines requires training:** uninformed use may cause injury. Never tie yourself into either end of a line without a reliable quick-release system. Have a knife ready to deal with unexpected entanglement. Learn to place set lines effectively, to throw accurately, to belay effectively, and to properly handle a rope thrown to you.

6. **When reviving a drowning victim,** be aware that cold water may greatly extend survival time underwater. Victims of hypothermia may have depressed vital signs so they look and feel dead. Don't give up; continue CPR for as long as possible without compromising safety.

V. UNIVERSAL RIVER SIGNALS

STOP: Potential hazard ahead. Wait for "all clear" signal before proceeding, or scout ahead. Form a horizontal bar with your outstretched arms. Those seeing the signal should pass it back to others in the party.

HELP/EMERGENCY: Assist the signaller as quickly as possible. Give three long blasts on a police whistle while waving a paddle, helmet or life vest over your head. If a whistle is not available, use the visual signal alone. A whistle is best carried on a lanyard attached to your life vest.

ALL CLEAR: Come ahead (in the absence of other directions proceed down the center). Form a vertical bar with your paddle or on one arm held high above your head. Paddle blade should be turned flat for maximum visibility. To signal direction or a preferred course through a rapid around obstruction, lower the previously vertical "all clear" by 45 degrees toward the side of the river with the preferred route. Never point toward the obstacle you wish to avoid.

VI. INTERNATIONAL SCALE OF DIFFICULTY

This is the American version of a rating system used to compare river difficulty throughout the world. This system is not exact; rivers do not always fit easily into one category, and regional or individual interpretations may cause misunderstanding. It is no substitute for a guidebook or accurate first-hand descriptions of a run.

Paddlers attempting difficult runs in an unfamiliar area should act cautiously until they get a feel for the way the scale is interpreted locally. River difficulty may change each year due to fluctuations in water level, downed trees, geological disturbances, or bad weather. Stay alert for unexpected problems!

As river difficulty increases, the danger to swimming paddlers becomes more severe. As rapids become longer and more continuous, the challenge increases. There is a difference between running an occasional Class IV rapid and dealing with an entire river of this category. Allow an extra margin of safety between skills and river ratings when the water is cold if the river itself is remote and inaccessible.

THE SIX DIFFICULTY CLASSES:

Class I: Easy. Fast moving water with riffles and small waves. Few obstructions, all obvious and easily missed with little training. Risk to swimmers is slight; self-rescue is easy.

Class II: Novice. Straightforward rapids with wide, clear channels which are evident without scouting. Occasional maneuvering may be required, but rocks and medium-sized waves are easily missed by trained paddlers. Swimmers are seldom injured and group assistance, while helpful, is seldom needed.

Class III: Intermediate. Rapids with moderate, irregular waves which may be difficult to avoid and which can swamp an open canoe. Complex maneuvers in fast current and good boat control are often required; large waves or strainers may be present but are easily avoided.

Strong eddies and powerful current effects can be found, particularly on large-volume rivers. Scouting is advisable for inexperienced parties. Injuries while swimming are rare; self-rescue is usually easy but group assistance may be required to avoid long swims.

Class IV: Advanced. Intense, powerful but predictable rapids requiring precise boat handling in turbulent water. Depending on the character of the river, it may feature large, unavoidable waves and holes or constricted passages demanding fast maneuvers under pressure. A fast, reliable eddy turn may be needed to initiate maneuvers, scout rapids, or rest. Rapids may require "must" moves above dangerous hazards. Scouting is necessary the first time down. Risk of injury to swimmers is moderate to high, and water conditions may make self-rescue difficult. Group assistance for rescue is often essential but requires practiced skills. A strong Eskimo roll is highly recommended.

Class V: Expert. Extremely long, obstructed, or very violent rapids which expose a paddler to above average endangerment. Drops may contain large, unavoidable waves and holes or steep, congested chutes with complex, demanding routes. Rapids may continue for long distances between pools, demanding a high level of fitness. What eddies exist may be small, turbulent, or difficult to reach. At the high end of the scale, several of these factors may be combined. Scouting is mandatory but often difficult even for experts. A very reliable Eskimo roll, proper equipment, extensive experience, and practiced rescue skills are essential for survival.

Class VI: Extreme. One grade more difficult than Class V. These runs often exemplify the extremes of difficulty, unpredictability, and danger. The consequences of errors are very severe and rescue may be impossible. For teams of experts only, at favorable water levels, after close personal inspection and taking all precautions. This class does **not** represent drops thought to be unrunnable, but may include rapids which are only occasionally run.

INDEX

ABOUT THE AMC

The Appalachian Mountain Club is where recreation and conservation meet. Our 37,000 members have joined the AMC to pursue their interests in hiking, canoeing, skiing, walking, rock climbing, bicycling, camping, kayaking, and backpacking, and—at the same time—to help safeguard the environment in which these activities are possible.

We invite you to join the Appalachian Mountain Club and share the benefits of membership. Every member receives *Appalachia Bulletin*, the membership magazine that, ten times a year, brings you listings of outdoor activities, workshops, excursions, volunteer opportunities, and news about environmental issues and AMC projects. Members are also eligible for discounts on AMC Books and maps, Education Workshops and Guided Hikes, and member rates at AMC Huts and Pinkham Notch Camp in New Hampshire, and Bascom Lodge in Massachusetts.

Since it was founded in 1876, the club has been at the forefront of environmental protection. By co-founding several of New England's leading environmental organizations, and working in coalition with these and many more groups, the AMC has influenced legislation and public opinion.

Volunteers in each chapter lead hundreds of outdoor activities and excursions, and offer introductory instruction in backcountry sports. The AMC Education Department offers members and the public a wide range of workshops, from introductory camping to the intensive Mountain Leadership School taught on the trails of the White Mountains.

The most recent efforts in AMC Conservation Programs include river protection, Northern Forest Lands policy, support for the American Heritage Trust, Sterling Forest (NY) preservation, and support for the Clean Air Act.

The AMC Research Department at Pinkham Notch Camp in New Hampshire focuses on the forces affecting the ecosystem, including ozone levels, acid rain and fog, climate change, rare flora and habitat protection, and air quality and visibility.

The AMC Volunteer Trails program, also based in Pinkham Notch and active throughout the AMC's twelve chapters, maintains over 1200 miles of trail, including 350 miles of the Appalachian Trail.

The club operates eight alpine huts in the White Mountains for hikers that provide shelter, bunks and blankets, and hearty meals. Pinkham Notch Camp, at the foot of Mount Washington, is base camp to the adventurous, and the ideal location for individuals and families new to outdoor recreation. Comfortable bunkrooms, mountain hospitality, and the home-cooked, family style meals make Pinkham Notch Camp a fun and affordable choice for lodging.

At AMC headquarters in Boston, the bookstore and information center stock the entire line of AMC Books, as well as other trail and river guides, maps, reference materials, and the latest articles on conservation issues. Knowledgeable AMC staff are always ready to answer your questions and help you get active in the outdoors.

Membership in the Appalachian Mountain Club provides vital support for our Conservation Programs. No matter why you're drawn to the outdoors—to hike and canoe, or to sketch and bird watch—you'll benefit from the AMC's efforts to protect our natural environment and teach responsible recreation.

Yes, I want to join the AMC.

Name _____ Home Phone _____

Address _____ Work Phone _____

City _____ State_____Zip _____

___ $40 Individual   ___ $65 Family

I enclose: ___ Check   ___ Visa/MasterCard
Account No. _____Exp. date _____
Signature _____

Mail payment and completed form to:
Appalachian Mountain Club, 5 Joy Street, Boston, MA 02108
Phone: (617) 523-0636   Fax: (617) 523-0722